The Book of Sc

By

S. L. Coyne

Published by Aranon Publishing - United Kingdom

www.AranonPublishing.com

Copyright © S. L. Coyne and Aranon Publishing 2017. All rights reserved.

ISBN: 978-0-244-31689-1

FIRST EDITION

For the purposes of all permissions licenses and agreements relating to this publication the written permission of the copyright owners or their designated agents must be in hard copy form and not electronic. Emails are not considered valid and will be classed as null and void for legal purposes. Any prior arrangements to excerpt use or quote this material is hereby rescinded under the new copyright ownership and new digital formats of the material. No part of this book may be reproduced in any form. This book is licensed to the purchaser for personal use only with all rights reserved.

No part of this publication may be reproduced or stored in a retrieval system, copied, duplicated or transmitted in any form, or by any means, electronic, mechanical, photocopying, recording,

internet, computer or used for presentation and demonstration purpose or otherwise without the express prior written permission of all copyright owners or in the case of reprographic production, in accordance with the terms of licenses issued by the Copyright Licensing Agency.

No part of this material may be used for excerpt purposes without the prior written permission of the copyright owners and any references to this publication must be accompanied by proper reference and due credit must be given to both the source www.AranonPublishing.com the publication and the copyright owners.

No part of this publication may be circulated in any form or binding or cover other than that in which it is published and without a similar condition being imposed on the subsequent purchaser.

Aranon Publishing - United Kingdom
http://www.AranonPublishing.com

DISCLAIMER

The material contained in this book is for information purposes only, being esoteric in nature. It is not intended to be a medical guide or a manual for self-treatment. The information represented in this book is not intended to be a substitute for medical counselling or treatment prescribed by your doctor. It is not intended to diagnose, treat or cure any disease or treat any individual's mental health problems or ailments.

This book is sold with the understanding that the publisher and the author are not liable for the misconception, misinterpretation or misuse of any information provided.

In the event you use any of the information in this book for yourself, which is your constitutional right, the publisher and author assume no responsibility for your actions with respect to any loss, damage, or injury caused or alleged to be caused directly or indirectly by the information contained in this book.

The intent of the author is only to offer the information contained in this book to help you in your quest for information about the subject.

If you have, suspect to have or are suspected of having a medical problem, we advise that you seek competent professional medical advice and assistance.

Books by S. L. Coyne

Rainbow Child

99 Ways to Rid Yourself of Toxic Relationships

Numinosity

The Omega Letters

The Book of Scrolls:

A Language of Angels

Inspirational Daily Guides from

Your Angel

By

S. L. Coyne

Contents

Introduction

Learning to Communicate with Angels

The White Code of Protection

Bibliomancy

Promise, Prayer, Poetry

Books of the Bible

Passages of the Bible Used

The Book of Psalms

Introduction

Humans have always been guided by beings they could not see or understand. We have been inspired to create such wonder and beauty that at times of strife, when we gaze upon such truth, we cannot believe it came from us. We are inspired, and we are guided everyday but do not realise. The paths we take, the commute we travel, the work we do is a well-kept road of possibilities from our own guides.

They have had many names through the ages but the one we are all familiar with is Angels. These beings from a higher plane of existence guide us through our trials and tribulations. We do not make mistakes even though it feels like it at times. No, our mistakes the angels believe, are nothing more than experiences no matter how painful or traumatic. Some people ask why. It is not that the universe picking on them. It is because they are stronger than anyone else and therefore can endure much more than an average human being.

"Mistakes are nothing more than experiences."

At times, these beings have inspired humans to write down their words and in so doing we have many beautiful pieces of work. Many of the books from the Bible can be argued, may have been written by humans but were inspired by the beings of light. Angelic intervention is part of our human world. We are after all beings of light ourselves.

"On the second day, God created the angels, with their natural propensity to good. Later, He made beasts with their animal desires. But God was pleased with neither. So, He fashioned man, a combination of angel and beast, free to follow good or evil."

Midrash (Hebrew Text)

Some social scientists and sociologists argue that our society is decaying because of the destruction of religious establishment intervention. It is true, that every ten-year census shows more and more of us no longer attend church. God is an unknown entity in our high powered super information highway world.

After all, who needs God when we have the internet?

However, what the sociologists do not understand is, just because established religion is dying in the Western world, spiritual belief is gaining ground. The spiritual truth that pulls at every human heart questions faith every day. The same questions we asked our Priests and Saints centuries ago, we now ask ourselves and find the answers to those questions ourselves.

We realise the truth and the divine lies within each of us. The angelic intervention we feel becomes ever more important and powerful for they bring us closer to the source than any church could. That source, that higher power is the inspiration and the divine that leads us home to the origin. To the origin of knowledge that is the beginning and the end; the alpha and omega.

We may have lost our established religions but we have gained a far greater truth for we now seek the knowledge within ourselves.

The Book of Scrolls is derived from texts which owe their origin to divine inspiration. There are words of inspiration from many of the books found in the Bible, the list of books and chapters can be found at the end of this book. Many of the pieces of poetry have been inspired by those texts. These beautiful words come from many different traditions and from many different people living centuries ago and a world away from us living today. Though we no longer attend church or sing these hymns or recite these words of inspiration, should they be lost to generations simply because we no longer go to church?

Yet we believe and we always will believe. We suffer the same as our grandparents and great grandparents. There is always war but the promise of peace is always present. There are always hardships whether financial, career, health, or with love. At these times, we question ourselves and the choices we made but remember there are no mistakes only experiences. Therefore, no matter how difficult these times are, we are not alone as all we need to do is ask for guidance and allow ourselves to feel the response from our angelic guides.

This book stems from a box of scrolls which was passed down from generation to generation. It has survived two world wars, countless moves and accompanied a small boy who travelled alone on a train to the countryside escaping bombs which dropped on London during the blitz. The box of scrolls is over a hundred years old and contains some 150 scrolls which are small and our now faded.

The words of inspiration and guidance find their way into the hearts of those who seek help. Those words written on the scrolls now find their way into this book.

To help us find their meaning and to gain further insight from them the addition of correspondences can be found on each page along with an interpretation for you to think on and contemplate. When we begin to finally open our eyes and see the divine within ourselves we also begin to see it in others. We see the divine in everything and we realise how interconnected everything is. The oils, crystals, and incense form a part of a ritual which you can create for yourself along with your angelic guides. It is when we understand the interconnectedness of all that we begin to truly learn the language of angels.

Learning to Communicate with Angels

As with all forms of communication a common language must be learnt. When we are communicating with beings that are as old as the earth and who speak all the languages of earth and of heaven, finding a common tongue can be difficult. That is why correspondences are so important as each sacred oil, incense or crystal resonates with an energy felt on a vibrational angelic level. These words which were once spoken by divine tongues still resonate with that energy.

However, we live in a world of duality therefore everything has its opposite and just as we communicate with beings of light there are angels of the dark also. It is paramount that we begin our conversations within a protective shield do not leave yourself open to attack from negativity. The best way to remember this is to think of a White Code of Protection.

WHITE CODE of PROTECTION

When beginning to work with angels it is important to coat yourself in protection. Think of protection as this:

* **P**ositive Thought

* **R**espect

* **O**mnipotence

* **T**rust

* **E**arth

* **C**all

* **T**ranscend

* **I**mmanence

* **O**rder

* **N**egative

Positive Thought

Think in a positive way. You may be experiencing negative aspects in your life but when beginning your communication with the angelic host you need to be in a positive state of mind. All the woes and worries of the day need to be cleared clean away. You maybe communicating with the beings of light for those problems but do not allow those worries to way you down.

Think positively as all will be well and everything will work out for the best. But you need to think it and feel it. Do not allow any form of negativity to manifest itself into a potential problem and unconsciously invoke a darker being.

Respect

Remember you are working with a 'celestial power that is higher in the evolutionary scale than we are.

We approach our angelic work with knowledge and reverence by taking courses in the angels your knowledge will grow. As a result, the respect will develop along with your deeper knowledge of the Psalms.

Omnipotence

Following on from the Respect and knowledge of angels comes the realisation that angels are also on the evolutionary scale and therefore there is a power higher than them. That Higher Power us everywhere and in everyone, it is a part of all. It is the connection and it is the divine. It is a spiritual umbilical cord that at certain times in our lives pulls us closer to it. Along that cord are the angels who can help us but they too are connected to us as is everything. In our learning of Angels, the Psalms for example may have the term Lord or God within it. You can omit the term for the correct corresponding angel. But always be aware of the unquestionable omnipotence of the Divine.

Trust

The belief and complete trust in yourself is paramount when communicating with angels. Your faith and trust in yourself ensures positive thought. Your confidence and belief in yourself releases the energy that resonates throughout the universe. Therefore, the result will be a positive outcome. Angels help with our problems but our belief and faith in ourselves must prevail. Trust in yourself, Trust in your instincts and Trust your angels in the final outcome of your problem or question.

Trust is a very difficult gift to accept especially in ourselves within a world when we are bombarded with so much self-doubt and worry. Yet remember these are negative emotions which can help to invoke those forces we do not want to work with. So, trust in yourself and believe.

Earth

Though we too are spiritual we are present on the earth plane. Therefore, we must also care for the earth as she too is a part of that spiritual cord which connects all beings. We are here on earth for a very short term compared to the angels. We are earth bound and our roots are within the earth though we are naturally aware of the spiritual within us.

When communicating using the language of angels it helps to ground us when we imagine that our feet are still here on earth embedded deep within the earth like tree roots. The image of earth brings us home when we communicate with the higher beings of light.

Call

We are connecting to the angels. We are calling to them using their language which is found in certain texts of the Bible found in the scrolls. We ask them in our call for help, guidance and support depending on our need. We make a call to the angelic host using the right language and correspondences which connects all throughout the universe including earth and heaven.

Transcend

When we all the angels using the White Code of Protection we need to be aware of the transcendental quality of that communication. We may feel it on the physical, spiritual or emotional level.

In the physical we may experience the hairs on our arms standing to attention. We may also feel tingling sensations throughout our bodies. We may even feel slightly nauseous or dizzy that everything is spinning and this is where our visualisation of our roots embedded in the earth helps to ground us.

On the spiritual level, we may feel in ourselves that we could fly. That our spirit can astral project to communicate with the angels on a higher level. While on the emotional level we could burst into tears or cry with laughter.

These are all possible reactions we can encounter when we begin to communicate with angels on a higher plane. These experiences are normal and not to be feared. This is our first contact. Transcend helps us to be aware of the potential experiences we can have.

Immanence

Immanence is to believe in the greater good. The belief that the work you do is for the greater good. Every form of communication with your angel is for the greater good. The positive thoughts in your heart and mind resonate within this immanence of the greater good which is everywhere and in everything. The Immanence is to believe in the greater good and its power throughout the universe.

Order

As you begin to communicate with your angels you will begin to learn that there is an order running through the angelic realm.

There are many levels of angels which are all responsible for the many different things that can affect our lives. There is an order and structure in everything on earth and so to in Heaven and indeed the entire universe.

Negative

As we began our White Code of Protection with positivity and positive thought we end this code with its direct opposite of Negativity. This is the universal law of duality, and remember every request that is not in the Light will be answered by its corresponding frequency of darkness. Remember there are Angels of Light and Angels of Darkness, and they are always malevolent no matter how clever they are at trickery.

Remember if your wish is in any way evil it will not be an Angel of Light who answers your call, regardless of the name you invoke but one of darkness.

Also remember Immanence before praying to any angel and ask yourself what motivates you and whether your motive is for the Greater Good, the Immanence that is found throughout the universe. The Good that resonated from you with your positive thought.

The main way to communicate with your angels safely is the appropriate way. It is also the way to combat the negative energies that may attack. The main way is through you with positive thinking. Everything you must be for the greater good.

"Search me, O God, and know my heart."
Psalm 139:23

In your heart is the greater good. Your thoughts towards the benefit to all living beings. Feelings within the heart is good and pure resonate a higher frequency for the light beings to feel and therefore answer your call. If you feel at any time there is some 'interference' from a negative energy. A fleeting moment of jealousy, covertness, anger, and hate towards someone then the counter part of your Heavenly angel has found a way in. Call upon your own guardian angel to rid yourself of this negative thought or feeling thereby destroying the connection the negative angel has. Recite Psalm 17

"Hear the right, O Lord, attend unto my cry, give ear unto my prayer, that goeth

not of feigned lips.

2 Let my sentence come forth from thy presence; let thine eyes behold the

things that are equal.

3 Thou hast proved mine heart; thou hast visited me in the night; thou hast

tried me, and shalt find nothing; I am purposed that my mouth shall

not transgress.

4 Concerning the works of men, by the word of thy lips I have kept me from

the paths of the destroyer.

5 Hold up my goings in thy paths, that my footsteps slip not.

6 I have called upon thee, for thou wilt hear me, O God: incline

thine ear unto me and hear my speech.

7 Shew thy marvellous lovingkindness, O thou that savest by thy right hand them which put their trust in thee from those that rise up against them.

8 Keep me as the apple of the eye, hide me under the shadow of thy wings.

9 From the wicked that oppress me, from my deadly enemies, who compass me about.

10 They are enclosed in their own fat; with their mouth, they speak proudly.

11 They have now compassed us in our steps: they have set their eyes bowing down to the earth;

12 Like as a lion that is greedy of his prey, and as it were a

young lion lurking in secret places.

13 Arise, O Lord, disappoint him, cast him down: deliver my soul from the wicked, which is thy sword;

14 From men which are thy hand, O Lord, from men of the world, which have their portion in this life, and whose belly thou fillest with thy hid treasure: they

are full of children, and leave the rest of their substance to their babes.

15 As for me, I will behold thy face in righteousness: I shall be satisfied, when I awake, with thy likeness.

Then recite verse 8 four times:

"Hide me under the shadow of thy wings."

As you recite this line four times imagine your angel of the Heavenly host shielding you from the negativity and evil under their wings.

If at any time throughout your communication with angels you feel there is some interference from an outside negative force trying to weasel their way in. Use this clearing and cleansing ritual to cut the tie between you and the fallen.

Further, you could always ask the 'angel' for their name as no fallen likes to divulge that information. The names of the angels are powerful forces in themselves. There are 150 Psalms and each one has an angel attached to it. However, there are many more Heavenly angels but always remember for every Light being there is its counterpart in the dark. The oldest system of opposites prevails: duality.

To learn how to communicate safely with the angels begins with you. The positive thought that resonates from you is a powerful force in itself. However, there are some extra positive powers that we find around everywhere and every day. The main form of protection is salt. Salt is an embodiment of the four elements on earth. Salt can be found in the sea, it is water. It can also be mined from the earth but both are dried within the air. When you place salt on your tongue it can burn therefore it is also fire.

There are also specific crystals you may want to use; Angel Opal or Opal Aura, Angelite, or Anglesite.

Angel Opal

This is crystal is a beautiful iridescent pearly opal which gives the impression of rainbows dancing within it. Each piece of Angel Opal is said to contain its own angel. It is a healing stone and especially beneficial to disorders of the nervous system.

Angelite

This crystal is a beautiful celestial blue colour. It is a healing stone and helps to connect with your guardian angel. It can also act as psychic shield against a negative person who wishes to harm you. Carry this crystal in your purse or wallet or keep a piece of it at work if you are being 'attacked' by negative co-workers.

Anglesite

This crystal is an almost colourless crystal which can have yellow, blue, or green flecks streaming through it. Anglesite is a powerful spiritual crystal which helps any form of meditation or connection with angels. It can also be used for spirit rescue if there is a presence in the house. It is a very powerful stone which should only be used or in plain sight when communicating with angels. Ideally it is a crystal to be used only with Archangel communication and after use wrapped in a cloth and stored away. Always wash your hands after handling Anglesite and keep away from pets.

The other form of protection that you need to be aware of is the time. All the Psalms are to be used in the daylight unless otherwise specified. In the Northern hemisphere, it can be difficult to decide when night begins as in winter it gets dark so early. During the day, the Heavenly angelic host have dominion while at night the fallen hold sway. Do not attempt to contact angels using the Psalms past 9pm until 7pm. There are certain times at night when the fallen have their most power and it is between 3am until 4am. If you find yourself being woken at 3.13am or anytime between 3am and 4am, recite Verse 8, 'Hide me under the shadow of Thy wings.' Then during the day perform the cleansing ritual using the full Psalm 17.

Bibliomancy

The intended way in which to use this book is very similar to the art of Bibliomancy. Since the beginning of time humans have sought ways to answer questions and delve deeper into the mysteries of consciousness to discover hidden truths.

The art of writing was regarded as something magical and wondrous. The divine written word held answers to all the questions humans ever asked. The books of the Bible yielded divine truths and Priests, Popes and monks would use this knowledge to settle disagreements. The art of Bibliomancy was born.

Bibliomancy involves the person asking a question, thinking on it, closing their eyes and then opening the Bible and whichever passage their hand touched that was the answer.

Another way the church used it was to choose a book which is believed to hold truth, balance it on its spine and then allowing the book to fall open on whatever page. However, the particular passage is always picked with the eyes closed.

Bibliomancy is a form of divination that has been passed down from generations and different peoples. It is no different from the auguries of ancient Rome and Greece when the flight of birds or the formation of clouds were interpreted to give answers to questions.

This Book of Scrolls can be used in that way but it can also be used to give hope and comfort when needed by simply opening a page at random and reading the words. If you wish to work with your angels on the passages then use the correspondences written. The meaning of the verses is determined by the original author written thousands of years ago yet it is discovered by readers of every age. Today, our goal must be exegesis or drawing the meaning out of the text and not eisegeses or superimposing a meaning onto the text, only you know how or what the text is saying.

The Guide for the Day is there only as a guide to help you make the most of the day and perhaps help you make a decision or answer a question.

Ask your angels for help and guidance, close your eyes and then open the page. Read the promise, prayer and poem which is given just for you by your angels.

There is also another way to use this book and that is creating your own prayers from it. At times, we may not know how to pray or what exactly to say. The poems can be placed together to create a message or prayer just for you. For example, this is a prayer of travelling created from different poems within the book:

Travelling Prayer

Heavenly Father, hear my prayer,

Hear my plea,

For I am a wanderer,

In search of Thee.

I looked at Jesus and I found

In Him my star, my sun;

And in that of life I'll walk

Till travelling days are done.

Walk in the light, thy path shall be

Peaceful, secure and bright;

For God by grace still dwells in thee,

And God himself is light.

Now the Spirit long neglected,

Waits with love before unknown;

And the Saviour, long rejected,

Claims and seals thee for his own.

Guide and save me from this strife,

Oh, heavenly Father help me in this life.

Amen.

There are many ways in which this book can be used but it is entirely up to you dear reader. As it is for you this book has been written and the reason why the scrolls have been given life again. These words of hope, comfort and joy cannot be forgotten and lost to generations for the power and energy that resonates within them can still be felt. The angels that inspired them still walk beside us and wait for us to call to them again. We merely have to ask and they will answer.

Enjoy the Book of Scrolls and feel the connection.

Though I walk in the midst of trouble, Thou wilt revive me.
Psalm 138:7

Leave me not, neither forsake, O God of my Salvation.
Psalm 27:9

He grants us for our tears
His oil of gladness;
Delivers, heals, and cheers,
Dispels all sadness.

Crystal: Lapis Lazuli
Colour: Blue
Oil: Lotus

Guide of the Day:
Do not be despondent and sad. Think of all the good things in your life. Make a list of all the positive things you can including things you take for granted such as being able to read and write, to see colours, and to feel the wind and rain on your face. Remember there is always hope.

I will not leave you comfortless; I will come to you.
John 14:18

I have loved thee with an everlasting love.
Jeremiah 31:3

When sore the combat, sharp the strife,
These words renew my strength and life -
Thou yet shalt more than conqueror prove,
Love with an everlasting love.

Crystal: Rose Quartz
Colour: Pink
Oil: Rose

Guide of the Day:
You are not alone. You are surrounded by so much love whether family and friends. If you are lonely for physical contact join a gym, take a night class and make new friends.

Fear thou not for I am with thee.
Isaiah 41:10

I am Thine, save me.
Psalm 119: 94

With Thee, O my God, for my Guardian
and my Guide,
Everywhere present and close by my side.

Crystal: Tree Agate
Colour: Green
Oil: Peppermint

<u>Guide of the Day:</u>
You may feel that you are in danger. So, take stock of where you are and where you going. Make sure you check everything and remember your angels are only a call away.

And they shall be my people and I will be their God.
Jeremiah 24:7

In the shadow of His hand hath He hid me.
Isaiah 49:2

For see the waning night is waning fast,
The breaking mourn is near;
And Jesus comes with voice of love,
The drooping soul to cheer.

Crystal: Carnelian
Colour: Orange
Oil: Vanilla

Guide of the Day:
Ask for what you truly want. Make a wish and send forth your desires. The universe will hear and will answer. Have faith and believe in yourself.

For this God is our God, for ever and ever.
Psalm 48:14

Lead me, O Lord, in Thy righteousness.
Psalm 5:8

Strong in the Lord of Hosts,
And in His mighty power,
Who in the strength of Jesus trusts,
Is more than conqueror.

Crystal: Clear Quartz
Colour: White
Oil: Spikenard

Guide of the Day:
You may feel ineffective when trying to assert yourself and that you have lost direction. But you are ready and stronger than you have ever been. Go for it!

He which hath begun a good work in you will perform it.
Philippians 1:6

Give ear to my words, O Lord; consider my meditations.
Psalm 5:1

And He who through the sinking flesh
The spirit's will can read,
Smiles on His work and sends again
All grace to meet my need.

Crystal: Jade
Colour: Green
Oil: Peppermint

Guide of the Day:
This time will pass as all days will pass. There is always tomorrow and no matter how bleak today has been the sun is going to shine tomorrow.

If we suffer we shall also reign with Him.
2 Timothy 2:12

I will freely sacrifice unto Thee.
Psalm 54:6

Who Suffer with Thee Lord below
Shall reign with Thee above;
Their glory and theirs to know;
The mystery of love.

Crystal: Turquoise
Colour: Turquoise Blue
Oil: Sage

Guide of the Day:

Show people what you are made of today. Show them you are a leader among all of them. Think about the way you present yourself to others and become the leader you are.

And there shall be no might there.
Revelations 22:5

O satisfy us early with Thy mercy; that we may rejoice and be glad all over our days.
Psalm 90:14

Fain, would I strike the gold harp,
And wear the promised crown,
And at Thy feet, while bending low,
Sing what Thy love has done.

Crystal: Apache Gold
Colour: Yellow
Oil: Sandalwood

<u>Guide of the Day:</u>
The end of a story is unfolding and tomorrow will bring a brighter day.

My people shall dwell in quiet resting places.
Isaiah 32:18

Return, O Lord; deliver my soul.
Psalm 6:4

When sore afflictions press me down,
I need Thy quickening powers,
The Word that I have rested on
Shall help my heaviest hours.

Crystal: Azezulite
Colour: White/Ivory
Oil: Chamomile

Guide of the Day:

Search for ways that bring about the inner expansion of your soul. The restlessness you feel is your inner self telling you to expand your learning.

The Lord redeemeth the soul of his servants.
Psalm 34:22

Let my heart be sound in Thy statutes; that I be not ashamed.
Psalm 119:80

Singing of Jesus, my blessed Redeemer,
God of the pilgrim, of Thee will I sing,
When o'er the billows of time I am wafted,
Still with Thy praise shall eternity ring.

Crystal: Septarian
Colour: Brown
Oil: Bergamot

Guide of the Day:
Tackles the old problems of the past today and put a spring in your step. There are new possibilities that you need to say yes to.

The Lord shall help them and deliver them.
Psalm 37:40

Now I pray to God that ye do no evil.
2 Corinthians 13:7

No earthly father loves like Thee,
No mother half so mild
Bears and forbears as Thou has done,
With me, Thy sinful child.

Crystal: Haematite
Colour: Silver/Grey
Oil: Dragon's Blood

Guide of the Day:
We all do the wrong things and say the wrong things but let your sense of humour out and laugh at yourself once in a while. Life is grand and crazy so just live it.

Thou wilt make all his bed in his sickness.
Psalm 41:3

O Lord, I am oppressed; undertake for me.
Isaiah 38:14

Child of God, has sickness laid thee
On a weary bed of pain?
He who chastens, He has saved thee;
Thy Father's grace will thee sustain.

Crystal: Healer's Gold
Colour: Gold
Oil: Myrrh

Guide of the Day:

Make sure you are looking after yourself today. Make that doctor, dentists, optician appointment. Have a check up and make sure all is good before you begin a new phase in your life.

He shall preserve thy soul.
Psalm 121:7

The God of all grace. Who hath called unto His eternal glory by Christ Jesus.
1 Peter 5:10

When sins and years prevailing rise,
To Thee I breathe my soul's desires.

Crystal: Blue Tiger's Eye
Colour: Navy Blue
Oil: Basil

Guide of the Day:
You have the ability to articulate who you are and your individualistic views with charm and personal magnetism. Do not doubt yourself.

Ask and ye shall receive, that your joy may be full.
John 16:24

Thou hast in love to my soul delivered it.
Isaiah 38:17

And make me feel it was my sin,
As though no their sins there were,
That was to Him who bears the world,
A load that He could scarcely bear.

Crystal: Green Obsidian
Colour: Emerald Green
Oil: Cedarwood

Guide of the Day:
Do not fall into obsessive thinking or allow a serious mood to dominate. Take yourself out for a walk in the park and have an ice-cream. Become as a child once more and see the wonder in everything.

My God shall supply all your need.
Philippians 4:19

Rejoice the soul of Thy servant, for unto Thee O Lord do I lift up my soul.
Psalm 86:4

Beyond thy utmost wants
His love and power can bless,
To praying souls, He always grants
More than they can express.

Crystal: White Selenite
Colour: Silver
Oil: Jasmine

Guide of the Day:

Everything comes in its own time. Learn patience and perseverance, and you will always prevail.

And I will put my spirit within you, and ye shall keep my judgements.
Ezekiel 36:27

Cast me not away from Thy presence; and take not Thy Holy Spirit from me.
Psalm 51:11

Now the Spirit, long neglected,
Waits with love before unknown;
And the Saviour, long rejected,
Claims and seals thee for His own.

Crystal: Ulexite
Colour: White
Oil: Fennel

Guide of the Day:
While money and possessions are obvious measures of what you perceive yourself to be worth, you need to value what is inside as that is what employers see. Your potential so show them what you are truly worth.

The Lord is the portion of mine inheritance and of my cup.
Psalm 16:5

Lord, I have loved the habitation of Thy house.
Psalm 26:8

Walk in the light, thy path shall be
Peaceful, secure, and bright;
For God by grace still dwells in thee,
And God himself is light.

Crystal: Milky Calcite
Colour: Ivory
Oil: Lily of the Valley

<u>Guide of the Day:</u>
Tell love ones how much you love them today and make someone smile with your own happiness.

He delivered them out of their distresses.
Psalm 107:6

Cause me to hear Thy loving kindness in the morning.
Psalm 143:8

I'll tell how in my heaviest grief
He calms my soul to rest;
How He can give that heart relief
Which leans upon His breast.

Crystal: Citrine
Colour: Yellow
Oil: Lemon

Guide of the Day:
Your body is telling you to take time out and recharge even if your mind is telling you to carry on. You need time to reflect and be on your own.

Thy shoes shall be iron and brass; and as thy days, so shall thy strength be.
Deuteronomy 33:25

How precious also are Thy thoughts unto me, O God.
Psalm 139:17

Thou, my everlasting portion,
More than friend or life to me,
All along my pilgrim journey,
Saviour, let me walk with Thee.

Crystal: Carnelian
Colour: Orange
Oil: Orange

Guide of the Day:
You may be feeling vulnerable right now but you have all the necessary support around you. Trust in friends and family to help you reach decisions.

Thou bow shall be seen in the cloud.
Genesis 9:14

Make us glad according to the days wherein Thou has afflicted us.
Psalm 90:15

Trials must and will befall;
But with humble faith to see
Love inscribed upon them all-
This is happiness to me.

Crystal: Rainbow Quartz
Colour: White
Oil: Frankincense

Guide of the Day:
Take your time in getting to places today, so what if you arrive a couple minutes late, at least you arrive safely.

Behold, I have graven Thee upon the palms of my hands.
Isaiah 49:16

I will praise Thy name, O Lord.
Psalm 54:6

Mine is an unchanging love,
Higher than the heights above,
Deeper than the depths beneath,
Free and faithful, strong as death.

Crystal: Pearl
Colour: Silver
Oil: Magnolia

Guide of the Day:
Accept love what it is an emotion on a higher level. Believe in that someone the way they believe in you.

Thine eyes shall see the King in His beauty.
Isaiah 33:17

Lay not this sin to their charge; and when He had said this, He fell asleep.
Acts 7:60

Then ask me not to linger,
For I'm pressing on the road
That leads me to my home above,
The city of my God.

Crystal: Moldavite
Colour: Green
Oil: Cinnamon

Guide of the Day:
Do not make rash decisions today take the day to ponder everything and only when you are confident make that decision. If there is a shadow of doubt then do not do whatever it is.

The Lord is good, a stronghold in the day of trouble.
Nahum 1:7

I trust in the mercy of God for ever and ever.
Psalm 52:8

I know not what the future hath,
Of marvel or surprise,
Assured alone that life and death
His mercy underlies.

Crystal: Amazonite
Colour: Turquoise Green
Oil: Basil

Guide of the Day:
Allow yourself to be surprised today and marvel in the mystery and wonder of the universe.

The Lord will preserve us unto His heavenly kingdom.
2 Timothy 4:18

I have not hid Thy righteousness within my heart.
Psalm 40:10

My weary spirit faints
To reach the land I love,
The bright inheritance of saints,
The Jerusalem above.

Crystal: Rhodonite
Colour: Pink
Oil: Hyacinth

Guide of the Day:
Your long-term desires can become reality. Well done your hard work has paid off.

Ye shall receive a crown of glory that fadeth not away.
1 Peter 5:4

Father, into Thy hands I commend my spirit.
Luke 23:46

O happy band of pilgrims
Look upward to the skies,
Where such a light affliction
Shall win you such a prize.

Crystal: Rose Quartz
Colour: Pink
Oil: Rose

<u>Guide of the Day:</u>
Everything is about timing and now is not the right time. Be patient your time will come.

I will restore health unto thee, and I will heal thee of thy wounds.
Jeremiah 30:17

O spare me, that I may recover strength before I go hence.
Psalm 39:13

Lord, though Thou bend my spirit low,
Love only shall I see;
The very hand that strikes the blow
Was wounded once for me.

Crystal: Spirit Quartz
Colour: White
Oil: Myrrh

Guide of the Day:
If your self-belief has been bruised by life's twists and turns underneath it all your true self is still shining. Do not hold onto pain but grieve and then let go.

And I will deliver thee out of the hand of the wicked.
Jeremiah 15:21

I said, Lord be merciful unto me; heal my soul for I have sinned against Thee.
Psalms 41:4

Twas thus the blood was shed,
Twas thus the life was poured;
Thus, Mercy gained her diadem,
While justice sheathed her sword.

Crystal: Kornerupine
Colour: Blue
Oil: Juniper

Guide of the Day:
You need to bring balance to your life. You need to find a work and life balance. Think about what area of your life needs more attention and set things in motion to restore the equilibrium.

Certainly, I will be with thee.
Exodus 3:12

Be not far from me, for trouble is near for there is none to help.
Psalm 22:11

Certainly, I will be with thee!
Let me feel it Saviour dear,
Let me know that art with me,
Very precious, very near.

Crystal: Rainbow Obsidian
Colour: Purple
Oil: Vervain

Guide of the Day:

At times, we can feel we are fenced in and unable to move in any direction. But there is always movement no matter how small. Begin to take baby steps to improve your situation and soon you will be running.

But the righteous into life eternal.
Mathew 25:46

At Thy right hand, there are pleasures for ever more.
Psalm 16:11

In that region sweetest flowers,
Fadeless, deathless, ever bloom;
There the joys that once were ours
Never wither in the tomb.

Crystal: Edenite
Colour: Grey
Oil: Bay

Guide of the Day:

The sky is no longer your limit for you are a star child so go forth today and shine.

I am the Lord thy God, the Holy one of Israel,
the Saviour.
Isaiah 43:3

I will work in Thy truth.
Psalm 86:11

Thus, may Thy word be dearer still,
And studied more each day;
And as it richly dwells within,
Thyself in it display.

Crystal: Aquamarine
Colour: Aqua
Oil: Lily

Guide of the Day:
You need to combine your heart's desire with your soul's purpose as then you will truly be complete.

Whosoever believeth in Him shall receive remission of sins.
Acts 10:43

For Thy Name's Sake, O Lord, pardon my iniquity, for it is great.
Psalms 25:11

His power subdues our sins,
And His forgiving love,
Far as the east is from the west,
Doth all our guilt remove.

Crystal: Desert Rose
Colour: Dusty Rose
Oil: Almond

Guide of the Day:

Knowledge and reverence are forces and strengths we all can have but you need to develop your knowledge further. Therefore, learn something new and attend a class in something you desire to learn.

For the Lord shall be thy confidence.
Proverbs 3:26

Arise, O Lord; save me, O my God.
Psalm 3:7

O how blessed are the moments,
When the Lord Himself draws near,
When I feel His gracious presence,
And He listens to my prayer.

Crystals: Lapis Lazuli
Colour: Navy Blue
Oil: Lotus

Guide of the Day:
Someone is keeping secrets from you but are you keeping secrets from them? Be open and honest and speak the truth from your heart.

Though he fall, he shall not be utterly cast down.
Psalm 37:24

Hide not Thy face from me in the day when I am in trouble.
Psalm 102:2

Let me be with Thee where Thou art,
My Saviour, my eternal rest;
There only will this longing heart
Be fully and for ever best.

Crystal: Spirit Quartz
Colour: Yellow
Oil: Apple Blossom

Guide of the Day:
If you have been feeling tired then have some rest and find time to have quiet moments to yourself. Relax and treat yourself to long soak in the bath or a day at a spa.

The salvation of the righteous is of the Lord.
Psalm 37: 39

Restore unto me the joy of Thy Salvation.
Psalm 51:12

Come now and view the Lamb of God,
Wounded and dead and bathed in blood!
Behold His side and venture near,
The well of endless life is here.

Crystal: Aventurine
Colour: Green
Oil: Basil

Guide of the Day:
Try to build firm foundations on which to base the future. You know what you need to do so go forth and make it happen.

Be of good comfort, thy faith hath made thee whole; go in peace.
Luke 8:48

I will trust in the covert of Thy wings.
Psalm 61:4

Heal us, Immanuel, here we are,
Waiting to feel Thy touch;
Deep wounded souls to Thee repair,
And, Saviour, we are such.

Crystal: Angelite
Colour: Lilac
Oil: Lilac

<u>Guide of the Day:</u>
Look out for the less fortunate today and help someone in need. At times people do not ask for help but offer it nevertheless.

His place of defence shall be the munitions of rocks.
Isaiah 33:16

Hear my prayer, O God; give ear to the words of my mouth.
Psalm 54:2

Thou art near - yes, Lord, I feel it,
Thou are near where'er I move;
And though sense would fain conceal it,
Faith oft whispers it in love.

Crystal: Blood Agate
Colour: Red
Oil: Hibiscus

Guide of the Day:
Go outdoors today and breath in the fresh air. Feel the sun on your skin and walk barefoot on the grass. Let the warmth of the sun heal your soul.

But unto you that fear my name shall the Sun of Righteousness arise with healing in His wings.
Malachi 4:2

Give ear to my prayer, O God.
Psalms 55:1

My Michael, He is the Angel of Angels,
He is the King of kings,
He is the Sun of Righteousness,
With healing in His wings.

Crystal: Obsidian
Colour: Purple
Oil: Sandalwood

Guide of the Day:
You have become established and independent because you are now in a position of decision making power. Be kind and act wisely as the leader you are.

For I am merciful saith the Lord.
Jeremiah 3:12

Into Thine hand I commit my spirit.
Psalm 31:5

Then murmur not, nor mourn,
My people faint and few;
Though earth to its foundations shake
My peace I leave with you.

Crystal: Laboradite
Colour: Blue
Oil: Juniper

Guide of the Day:
An opportunity may be coming your way. Act wisely and you can have everything you desire.

Who gave Himself for us that He might redeem
us from all iniquity.
Titus 2:14

Hide Thy face from my sins and blot out all
mine iniquities.
Psalm 51:9

My guilt is cancelled quiet, I know,
And satisfaction made;
But the vast debt of love I owe,
Can never be repaid.

Crystal: Ruby Star
Colour: Burgundy
Oil: Rose

<u>**Guide of the Day:**</u>
You may be daydreaming and building castles in the air. Dreams are all well and good but not when they stop you from getting your soul's desire.

I will take the stony heart out of your flesh, and
I will give you a heart of flesh.
Ezekiel 36:26

Incline my heart unto Thy testimonies and not
to covetousness.
Psalm 119:36

The mercy seat is open still,
There let my soul retreat,
with humble hope attend Thy will,
And wait beneath Thy feet.

Crystal: Green Fluorite
Colour: Light Green
Oil: Eucalyptus

Guide of the Day:
Be prepared to work hard to get what you want but at the same time you will also learn to become a great craftsperson.

To him that overcometh will I give to eat of the tree of life.
Revelations 2:7

But mine eyes are unto Thee O God the Lord; in Thee is my trust.
Psalm 141:8

Oh! Paradise is wondrous fair,
The angel's joyous home is there;
And all who trust in Jesus' blood
Shall reach the paradise of God.

Crystal: Celestite
Colour: Duck Egg Blue
Oil: Myrrh

Guide of the Day:
Try to be understanding at this time and learn to become the ruler of your own emotions. Try not to rush into any decisions.

He will fulfil the desire of them that fear Him.
Psalm 145:19

My Soul thirsteth for thee.
Psalm 63:1

Then faint not, and fear not, His presence is nigh,
His arm shall protect thee, His fulness supply.

Crystal: Blue Jade
Colour: Blue
Oil: Bluebell

<u>Guide of the Day:</u>
Don't waste time and energy concentrating on unimportant details. Try to see the bigger picture and always believe in yourself.

Surely goodness and mercy shall follow me all the days of my life.
Psalm 23:6

O Lord, upon Thou my lips; and my mouth shall show forth Thy praise.
Psalm 51:15

Have you not a word for Michael? Not a word for Him?
He is listening through the chorus of the burning Seraphim!

Crystal: Blood Stone
Colour: Dark Red
Oil: Ginger

Guide of the Day:
Someone of the past reminds you of childhood, think back on these days and smile but remember you are now living in the present. The past is alright to visit but you cannot remain there.

The Lord is my shepherd; I shall not want.
Psalm 23:1

I will call upon Thee, for Thou wilt answer.
Psalm 86:7

Jesus is our Shepherd, for the sheep he bled;
Every lamb is sprinkled with the blood He shed.

Crystal: Amethyst
Colour: Purple
Oil: Lavender

Guide of the Day:
You are full of ideas and creative thoughts so write them down and be stimulated by your fantastic thoughts.

The Lord shall preserve thee from all evil.
Psalm 121:7

For thou Lord wilt bless the righteous.
Psalm 5:12

My soul, ask what thou wilt
Thou canst not be too bold
Since His own blood for thee was spilt,
What else can He withhold?

Crystal: Sunstone
Colour: Orange
Oil: Honey

Guide of the Day:
Do not be afraid of the demons of the mind but at times these monsters must be met. Face up to your fears and confront them and the demons will disappear.

The eternal God is the refuge and underneath
are the everlasting arms.
Deuteronomy 33:27

God be merciful unto us and bless us, and
cause His face to shine upon us.
Psalm 67:1

When of human aid despairing,
And no voice the tempest calms,
Think of this, that underneath you,
Are the 'Everlasting Arms'.

Crystal: Chrysocolla
Colour: Turquoise-Blue
Oil: Orchid

Guide of the Day:
This world is full of competition and conflicting views but stand up for yourself and your ideas and refuse to be a victim.

I am the Lord which exercise loving-kindness.
Jeremiah 9:24

I delight to do Thy will, O my God.
Psalm 40:8

The wisest will is God's own will,
Rest on this anchor and be still,
For peace around thy path shall flow,
When only wishing here below - what pleases God.

Crystal: Smoky Quartz
Colour: Indigo
Oil: Patchouli

Guide of the Day:
At the core of your being is a sense of dissatisfaction this is a call for you to make the changes you have long desired. Start the day as you mean to go on.

If ye shall ask anything in my name, I will do it.
John 14:14

Lord, what wilt Thou have me to do?
Acts 9:6

Then let our humble faith address
His mercy and His power;
We shall obtain delivering grace
In the distressing hour.

Crystal: Meteorite Gibeon
Colour: Brown
Oil: Allspice

Guide of the Day:
At times, we are wronged by those we trust and we feel a sense of betrayal, but instead of wishing ill towards those who betrayed us have faith in Justice herself to prevail.

Behold the eye of the Lord is upon them that fear Him.
Psalm 33:18

Lord, Thou wilt ordain peace for us.
Isaiah 26:12

Thine eye, Thine ear, they are not dull,
Thine arm can shortened be
Behold me now, my heart is full,
Behold and undertake for me.

Crystal: Peridot
Colour: Olive Green
Oil: Lemon Balm

Guide of the Day:
Joy and happiness is celebrated today so enjoy the day with enthusiasm and invite all friends and family to partake of this special day too.

I will be their God and they shall be my people.
2 Corinthians 6:16

Lead me in the way everlasting.
Psalm 139: 24

In the refuge God provided,
Though the world's destruction lowers,
We are safe in Christ confided,
Everlasting life is ours.

Crystal: Citrine
Colour: Yellow
Oil: Lemon

Guide of the Day:
At times, we must sacrifice the present happiness for something we truly desire. There is always a lost and sacrifice is a part of life. This time will pass.

For all the promises of God in Him are Yea, and in Him Amen.
2 Corinthians 1:20

I shall not be moved.
Psalm 16:8

Come and rejoice with me,
For I have found a friend
Who knows my heart's most secret depth,
Yet loves me without end.

Crystal: Ametrine
Colour: Yellow
Oil: Bergamot

Guide of the Day:
At times, we need to be full of discipline in order to complete the tasks which are before us. Be full of strength and determination and go forward safe in the knowledge that you will prevail.

He that doeth the will of God abideth for ever.
John 2:17

I set my face unto the Lord God to seek Him by prayer and supplication.
Daniel 9:3

Alone with God; oh, sweet to me,
This covert to whose shade I flee,
To breathe repose in Thee - in Thee.

Crystal: Hessonite Garnet
Colour: Orange
Oil: Allspice

Guide of the Day:
You have all the power within and if you can change your mind you can change your world.

And they shall be mine, saith the Lord of Hosts,
in that day when I make up my jewels.
Malachi 3:17

Say unto my soul I am thy salvation.
Psalm 35:3

Like the stars of the morning,
His bright crown adorning,
They shall shine in their beauty,
Bright gems for His crown.

Crystal: Green Amazonite
Colour: Green
Oil: Mint

Guide of the Day:
The outcome you seek is unclear and someone is withholding the truth from you. Be on your guard around this person, chances are you already know them and already have your doubts regarding this person.

They shall mount up with wings as eagles.
Isaiah 40:31

My righteousness I hold fast and will not let it go.
Job 27:6

Foes in plenty we shall meet;
Hearts courageous scorn defeat;
So, we press with eager feet up and on.

Crystal: Ruby Star
Colour: Burgundy
Oil: Carnation

Guide of the Day:

Trust your instincts today. Believe what you are seeing as it is the truth and your eyes do not lie. Go with your gut instinct and trust your first thought.

Before they call I will answer.
Isaiah 65:24

Let my supplication, I pray Thee be accepted before Thee.
Jeremiah 37:20

Arise, my soul, from my deep distress,
And banish every fear;
He calls thee to His throne of grace
To spread thy sorrows there.

Crystal: Merlinite
Colour: Grey
Oil: Frankincense

Guide of the Day:
You were born to create and the world is your canvas so use the most vivid colours you can find to create your dreams. Express yourself through the many different forms of art.

And He knoweth them that trust in Him.
Nahum 1:7

Search me, O God, and know my heart.
Psalm 139:23

God is mighty to deliver,
None His power can withstand;
In all trial whatsoever,
He will be our gracious Friend.

Crystal: Falcon Eye
Colour: Blue
Oil: Honeysuckle

<u>Guide of the Day:</u>
A once in a lifetime opportunity is coming your way or has already presented itself to you and take the opportunity.

Be strong, all ye people of the land - and work;
for I am with you.
Haggai 2:4

Wash me thoroughly from mine iniquities and
cleanse one from my sin.
Psalm 51:2

From man and from ourselves we cease,
And rest on Thy Almighty arm;
Keep Thou our souls in constant peace,
And shelter us from every harm.

Crystal: Red Tiger's Eye
Colour: Red
Oil: Ginger

Guide of the Day:
You have the potential to become a great leader in your chosen field but always remember how you got there. Honour and respect those that helped you get where you are.

And they shall never perish.
John 10:28

And my mouth shall show forth Thy praise.
Psalm 51:15

O rejoice, Christ's happy sheep!
For your Shepherd will for ever
You, His flock, in safety keep;
You are objects of His favour.

Crystal: Clear Calcite
Colour: White
Oil: Jasmine

Guide of the Day:
If a storm arrives today do not worry as you have evaluated the situation and was ready for it. If it does not come to pass at least you are ready for the next storm which shall come. Storms always do but we can be ready for them.

So, shall we even be with the Lord.
1 Thessalonians 4:17

In God have I put my trust; I will not be afraid.
Psalm 56:11

In the blest realm of endless day
The Lamb shall all our wants supply;
And God's own hand shall wipe away
The falling tear from every eye.

Crystal: Leopardskin Jasper
Colour: Yellow
Oil: Fennel

Guide of the Day:

Choose your projects wisely and be careful not to put all your eggs in one basket.

I will put my fear in their hearts.
Jeremiah 32:40

Hold up my going in Thy paths.
Psalm 17:5

He richly feeds my soul
with blessing from above,
And leads me where the rivers roll,
of everlasting love.

Crystal: Jet
Colour: Black
Oil: Patchouli

<u>Guide of the Day:</u>
Every day is a beginning of a change. Every day is another step in our life's journey. No matter how powerful we are we cannot cease time from moving forward.

He shall give His angels charge over thee to keep thee in all thy ways.
Psalm 91:11

Teach my Thy way, O Lord, I will walk in Thy truth.
Psalm 86:11

The chief of sinners He receives;
His Saints He loves, and never leaves;
He'll guard us safe from every ill,
And all His promises fulfil.

Crystal: Rainbow Moonstone
Colour: Silver
Oil: Neroli

Guide of the Day:
Learn all you can about the gathering storm and be prepared. Have your knowledge stacked up to fight against the onslaught and release any energy you may have regarding the confrontational storm.

Thou art my hiding place; Thou shalt preserve
me from trouble.
Psalm 32:7

Hear my prayer, O Lord, and let my cry come
unto Thee.
Psalm 102:1

In the Rifted Rock I'm resting,
Sure, and safe from all alarm;
Storms and billows have united,
All in vain to do me harm.

Crystal: Shiva Lingam
Colour: Indigo
Oil: Bluebell

Guide of the Day:
All change is creative and change is as good as a rest. So, go forward with change.

Thou shalt compass me about with songs of deliverance.
Psalm 32:7

Before I was afflicted I went away: but now have I kept Thy word.
Psalm 119: 67

From all that dwell below to the skies
Let the Creator's praise arise;
Let the Redeemer's name be sung,
Through every land, by every tongue.

Crystal: Amber
Colour: Orange
Oil: Amber

Guide of the Day:
Release your negative emotions and let it all out. Better out than in as these emotions can turn toxic in a short space of time making you ill.

He shall give you another comforter that He may abide with you for ever.
John 14:16

I will pray the Father, and He shall give you another comforter.
John 14:16

This high glory we inherit,
This free gift through Jesus' blood,
God the Spirit with our spirit
Witnesseth we're sons and daughters of God.

Crystal: Flash Opal
Colour: Green
Oil: Basil

Guide for the Day:
Have you picked up the phone only to hear no one on the other end? These are all signs that your angels are around and want you to know that you will be o.k. Everything will be fine. Your angels and spirit guides may have a special message for you. It is always best to

hear messages in a dream. Keep a pen and note pad by the bed and ask before you go to sleep: "Do you have a message for me. Please come forward tell me in my dreams and in my sleep."

For in the Lord Jehovah is everlasting strength.
Isaiah 26:4

Stir up Thy strength and come and save us.
Psalm 80:2

I'll go in the strength of the Lord
In paths, He has marked for my feet;
I will follow the Light of His word,
Nor shrink from the dangers I meet.

Crystal: Ocean Jasper
Colour: Silver
Oil: Lavender

Guide of the Day:
Do not fear the dark. Do not fear the unknown. There is nothing in the dark that can hurt you only your own fears. So, embrace the dark and see the beauty of the stars and the universe around you.

The sun shall not smite thee by day nor the moon by night.
Psalm 121:6

For thou, Lord, only makest me dwell in safety.
Psalm 4:8

Did ever trouble thee befall,
And He refuse to hear thy call?
And has He not His promise passed,
That thou shalt overcome at last?

Crystal: Sunstone
Colour: Yellow
Oil: Mimosa

Guide of the Day:
A shock knocks us for six when we first hear it but then just as quickly as it came we begin to think what to do concerning it. You have all the tools to deal with this shock. This news has come to you for a reason or purpose as you are the only one who can handle this. You are the only one who can sort it. You are the strong,

dependable one who will deal with the effect of the shock and you will always prevail.

I am with thee, saith the Lord, to save thee.
Jeremiah 30:11

The Lord hath heard my supplication.
Psalm 6:9

Through waves and clouds and storms,
He gently cheers thy way;
Wait then He time, so shall the night
Soon end in joyous day.

Crystal: Rainbow Obsidian
Colour: The entire rainbow spectrum
Oil: Almond

Guide of the Day:
There may be a few bumps on the road but it is still a good sign but in a relationship or marriage these can become mountains. However, as it means whatever obstacles come your way as a couple you can overcome them. You are stronger together when you have to face a storm.

Thou, O God, hast prepared of Thy goodness for the poor.
Psalm 68:10

Incline Thine ear, O Lord.
Isaiah 37:17

We love the Lord, for He hath heard our crying,
His ear inclined to us in our distress;
And now on Him, with firmest trust relying,
In every danger to His throne we press.

Crystal: Smoky Quartz
Colour: Brown
Oil: Neroli

Guide of the Day:
Storms are inevitable and are on the way today. Do not live in fear of it, go forth and embrace the storm. Acknowledge the storm and marvel at its power.

Who crowneth thee with loving kindness and
tendor mercies.
Psalm 103:4

Thou crownest the year with Thy goodness.
Psalm 65:11

I see no step before me
As I tread the days of the year,
And the past is still in God's keeping,
The future His mercy shall clear.

Crystal: Carnelian
Colour: Orange
Oil: Jasmine

Guide of the Day:
Your true friends are around you and thinking of you. Pick up that phone and speak to them or write that letter and send it to them. We all need to our twin flames, we all need our Anam cara.

The Lord will give strength unto His people.
Psalm 29:11

I cried by reason of mine affliction who the Lord and He heard me.
Jonah 2:2

Lead, Saviour, lead amid the encircling gloom,
Lead Thou me on;
The night is dark and I am far from home,
Lead Thou me on.

Crystal: Blue Lace Agate
Colour: Blue
Oil: Rosemary

Guide of the Day:
Whatever plans you have put in place will come to fruition and you will be successful. You may need the help of others but you will be given all the credit for the success of your endeavour as without you this project would not have come to pass.

Be not afraid of their faces; for I am with thee to
deliver thee, saith the Lord.
Jeremiah 1:8

Who shall dwell in Thy holy hill.
Psalm 15:1

Jesus, I am sometimes weary
While I tread this dreary plain;
Let Thy gracious presence cheer me,
Then all loss I count but again.

Crystal: Angelite
Colour: White
Oil: Honeysuckle

Guide of the Day:
You may need professional advice or help but do not be afraid to ask for it as no one can take this project from you for it is well and truly yours. At times, we all need other professionals to help. We need outside positivity in our project. We need others to tell us what is needed.

Come unto me all ye that labour, and I will give
you rest.
Mathew 11:28

For thou hast been a strength to the poor.
Isaiah 25:4

I have no help but Thine, nor do I need
Another arm save Thine to rest upon;
It is enough, my Lord, enough indeed,
My strength us in Thy right, Thy might alone.

Crystal: Poppy Jasper
Colour: Red
Oil: Poppy

Guide of the Day:
Check travel plans, routes and plan ahead in case something goes wrong. Do you have everyone's' telephone number? There is also a warning for not only travel and the daily commute but also a warning for health. So, stop and have a check-up at the Doctors.

For He is my life and the length of thy days.
Deuteronomy 30:20

Teach me Thy way, O Lord, and head me in a plain path.
Psalm 27:11

Let me, my Saviour, on Thy breast recline
Thy words my comfort, my devotion Thine;
My life's best joy Thy promises to prove,
Trust un Thy truth, and triumph in Thy love.

Crystal: Tsarovite Garnet
Colour: Green
Oil: Geranium

Guide of the Day:

If you feel you are putting on weight do not go out and buy another size instead start a diet. These are all warning signs, when clothes get tight, when we cannot sleep, or when we feel tired all the time. It is time to take stock and take heed to the warning.

And God shall wipe away all tears from their eyes.
Revelation 21:4

Show me thy glory.
Exodus 33:18

Then God's own hand shall wipe the tear
From every weeping eye,
And pains, and sighs, and groans, and tears
Shall cease eternally.

Crystal: Apache Tear
Colour: Grey
Oil: Magnolia

Guide of the Day:
The universe has given you a great gift... life. So, use it. Make your dreams into reality. Do not put restraints and constraints around it. Just do it. You have a special gift called manifestation and you can use it well. Begin now to see your reality in the world around you.

His children shall have a place of refuge.
Proverbs 14:26

I have waited for Thy salvation, O Lord.
Genesis 49:18

O Jesus, to tell of Thy love
Our souls shall for ever delight,
And join with the blessed above
In praises by day and by night.

Crystal: Vanadinite
Colour: Red
Oil: Ginger

<u>Guide of the Day:</u>
Something you have desired for so long is now within your reach. All your plans and hard work have paid off and you are now successful.

The Lord they God hath chosen thee to be a special people unto Himself.
Deuteronomy 7:6

Grant thee according to thine own heart, and fulfil all thy counsel.
Psalm 20:4

Dear Saviour keep my spirit stayed,
Hard following after Thee,
Till in in robes of white arrayed,
Thy face of glory see.

Crystal: Infinite Stone
Colour: Green
Oil: Tarragon

Guide of the Day:
Have a clear out of clothes or things around your home and take to the charity shop. One man's rubbish is another man's treasure.

I will guide thee with mine eye.
Psalm 32:8

Speak, for Thy servant heareth.
1 Samuel 3:10

The thorn-crowned brow, with smitten Cheek,
O how they plead with thee!
His blistered feet also they speak
Be brave and follow me.

Crystal: Goldstone
Colour: Gold
Oil: Vervain

Guide of the Day:
You need to acknowledge your own fears and phobias. Learn to confront and overcome them as your fears are holding you back in a situation.

He that watereth shall be watered also himself.
Proverbs 11:25

Open Thou mine eyes, that I may behold wondrous things.
Psalm 119:18

I thirst, but not as once I did,
The vain delights of earth to share;
Thy wounds, Immanuel, all forbid
That I should find my pleasure there.

Crystal: White Celestite
Colour: White
Oil: Magnolia

Guide of the Day:
There is an interlaced pattern which will bring you some good news or a good opportunity. For example, a brother of a friend whose wife works at such and such says there is a vacancy for someone like you. It is these signs that interlaced and woven connections of human

relations that can lead to new potential possibilities.

I will instruct thee and teach thee in the way
that thou shalt go.
Psalm 32:8

I will both lay me down in peace and sleep.
Psalm 4:8

When I am feeble as a child,
And flesh and heart give way
Then on Thy everlasting strength
With passive trust, I say.

Crystal: Picasso Jasper
Colour: Cream
Oil: Patchouli

Guide of the Day:
Sometimes our best intentions do not come to pass and they fall through the net. If you can, pick yourself up and dust yourself off. If you cannot it may be wise in investing in some professional help to find the best possible way forward.

He hath said, I will never leave thee, nor forsake thee.
Hebrews 13:5

Strengthen me according unto Thy word.
Psalm 119:28

The soul that on Jesus hath leaned for response,
He'll never, no never, desert to its foes.

Crystal: Blue Halite
Colour: Indigo
Oil: Rosemary

Guide of the Day:
To all living beings on the earth including plants and trees feel the connection and show respect to them by doing a good deed for them no matter how small. So, water those plants and trim that hedge. Look out for nature and feel the connection.

All are yours, and ye are Christ's and Christ is God's.
1 Corinthians 3:22-23

Hide me under the shadow of Thy wings.
Psalm 17:8

Thrice happy whose souls are stayed
On Christ's unseen but certain aid;
Beneath His shadow they'll retreat,
And never fear afflicting heat.

Crystal: Violan
Colour: Violet
Oil: Lilac

Guide of the Day:
Friends and family all reach out to one another and need nurturing in some way. Like a mother who looks after her children. Make a Mother's Day every day for those who care for you. Send a card or a make a phone call to say hello and ask how they are.

Fear not, for I have redeemed thee; I have called thee by name.
Isaiah 43:1

Therefore, now let it please Thee to bless the house of Thy servant.
2 Samuel 7:29

Fling out the banner! Let it float
Skyward and seaward, high and wide,
Our gory, only in the cross;
Our only hope, the Crucified!

Crystal: Kornerupine
Colour: Blue
Oil: Juniper

Guide of the Day:
If you are alone in the world then you need the nurturing. Join a group, nurture your interests and go to night school. See where your interests will lead you. Nurture your soul and nurture you.

It is I; be not afraid.
Mathew 14:27

O Lord God, remember me, I pray Thee and strengthen me.
Judges 16:28

Mine eyes are watching near thy bed,
Mine arms are underneath thee spread,
My blessing is around thee shed;
"'Tis I, be not afraid."

Crystal: Isis Quartz
Colour: White
Oil: Lily of the Valley

Guide of the Day:
Do not force your dream into reality. Set the pieces in formation and watch it come to pass. You have to be active and manifest what you want but even with manifestation the final result will always depend upon the work of the universe. Just remember good things come to those who wait.

I know that whatsoever God doeth it shall be for ever.
Ecclesiastes 3:14

I will abide in Thy tabernacle for ever.
Psalm 61:4

We shall dwell with Christ for ever when the shadows flee away,
In the everlasting glory of the everlasting day.

Crystal: Fuchsite
Colour: Green
Oil: Anise

<u>Guide of the Day:</u>
You need patience for a project to unfold. Everything happens at the right time, no matter how much we want it now. We have to wait as everything in this world grows at its own pace and that includes dreams.

Surely, He shall deliver thee from the snare of the fowler.
Psalm 91:3

The Lord will receive my prayer.
Psalm 6:9

That were a grief I could not bear
Thou not hear and answer prayer;
But a prayer hearing answering God,
Supports me under every rod.

Crystal: Herderite
Colour: Pale Green
Oil: Myrrh

Guide of the Day:
You are a force to be feared as you will explode and destroy everything in your path, if you do not rid yourself of this person or item that is making you ill. You can feel yourself building up to an explosion and it is only a matter of time. Tell them to back off, and walk away before you become that force.

I will strengthen thee, yea, I will help thee.
Isaiah 41:10

But let all those that put their trust in Thee rejoice.
Psalm 5:11

Strengthen my hand, O Lord, for I am weak
Thou art the strong one, Lord, Thy help I seek.

Crystal: Verdite
Colour: Green
Oil: Lotus

Guide of the Day:
The guide for today means stay put and hold fast. Hold onto something tangible. Hold onto your reality and grip tight to your dreams. We cannot see beyond the dense fog which sweeps all around us. Stay put and do not make any moves such as selling the house or leaving a relationship until the fog has completely cleared and it will.

Thine path of the just is as the shining light that shineth more and more into the perfect day.
Proverbs 4:18

I will keep thy statutes.
Psalm 119:8

I looked at Jesus and I found
In Him my star, my sun;
And in that of life I'll walk
Till travelling days are done.

Crystal: Eudialyte
Colour: Purple
Oil: Hibiscus

<u>Guide of the Day:</u>
Follow the moon cycle and start a fresh. Go on a diet, give up smoking, do not drink alcohol this whole month and see how you feel after 28 days.

Even the night be light about me.
Psalm 139:11

Say unto my soul I am thy salvation.
Psalm 35:3

Sun of my soul, thou Saviour dear,
It is not night if thou be near
Oh! May no earth-born cloud arise,
To hide Thee from Thy servant's eyes.

Crystal: Rose Quartz
Colour: Pink
Oil: Rose

Guide of the Day:
There are big changes on the way that if resisted could be painful. Ask your angels for help and guidance to get through this.

No weapon that is formed against Thee shall prosper.
Isaiah 54:17

Teach me Thy way, O Lord, I will walk in Thy truth.
Psalm 86:11

May we to Thee in all our wants
Child-like yet closer fly,
Directing stull, throughout our course,
By faith to thee our eye.

Crystal: Rose Aura Quartz
Colour: Deep Pink
Oil: Cherry Blossom

Guide of the Day:
The desire to control everything has its time and place but right now you just have to let go of your own desires and accept what is before you. This time is a quick shower on your journey. Just because the rain has come does not mean you will lose your direction. If

anything, think of it as a brief respite and a rest from the hard work you have given yourself. Everything is nurtured from a little rain.

He shall save His people from their sins.
Mathew 1:21

For I acknowledge my transgression; and my sin is ever before me.
Psalm 51:3

I give Thee thanks unfeigned
O Jesus Friend in need
For what Thy soul sustained
When Thou for me didst bleed.

Crystal: Water Sapphire/Iolite
Colour: Violet
Oil: Hyacinth

Guide of the Day:
In our modern day and age, we can rush around here and there and never realise the damage we are doing ourselves. Do not fret over resting your mind, your body and soul needs it.

The voice of weeping shall be no more heard.
Isaiah 65:19

Thou Son of David have mercy on us.
Mathew 9:27

Oft I walk beneath the cloud
Dark as midnight's gloomy shroud;
But when fear is at its height
Jesus comes and all is light.

Crystal: Cat's Eye
Colour: Green
Oil: Catmint

Guide of the Day:
There are many roads to choose and you have many opportunities coming to you. Yet while others cannot see the forest for the trees you can clearly see your way out.

He that trusteth in the Lord, mercy shall
compass him about.
Psalm 32:16

It is good for me that I have been afflicted that I
might learn Thy statutes.
Psalm 119:71

The little worries which we meet each day
May lie as stumbling - blocks across our way
Or we may make them stepping - stones to be
Of grace, O Lord, to Thee.

Crystal: Amber
Colour: Orange
Oil: Orange

Guide of the Day:
Do not allow yourself to be deceived as there are those around you who would say one thing to your face and another behind your back. Find the truth out by yourself and believe no one till you have all the facts. Notice when words do not match actions. There is a lack of

harmony which could lead to a storm. You could be at the centre of it. Make sure you gain all insights.

Where I am, there shall also my servant be.
John 12:26

Give Thy strength unto Thy servant.
Psalm 86:16

Soon and for ever the soldier lays down
The sword for a harp and the cross for a crown.

Crystal: Carnelian
Colour: Orange
Oil: Marigold

Guide of the Day:
Look after your energy. You may have a sudden burst of energy at the moment or the opposite. At time in our lives it is hard to find the right balance between our energy levels. Whichever category you fall into at this moment in time keep a check of your energy levels. Make sure you are well rested and eat the right foods and of course drink plenty of water.

And my people shall dwell in a peaceable habitation.
Isaiah 32:18

Wash me thoroughly from mine iniquity.
Psalm 51:2

Let one his innocence glory
Another in works he has done -
The Blood is my claim and my title
Beside it, O Lord I have none.

Crystal: Prehnite
Colour: Green
Oil: Vervain

Guide of the Day:
You need to be more organised and regimented in your life both in your working life and personal life. Although we all need to be flexible and adaptable in many things we do also need to be more structured. Write lists, check our statements and bank balances. What goes out and what comes in.

In Thy presence is fulness of joy.
Psalm 16:11

Because He is at my right hand, I shall not be moved.
Psalm 16:8

Be Thou at my right hand
Then I shall never fail
Uphold Thou me and I shall stand;
Fight and I must prevail.

Crystal: Ulexite
Colour: White
Oil: Fennel

Guide of the Day:
Begin to clear out that which has run its course. Those things that are of no use. Tidy and organisation go together. Start with one room of the house or one area of your life and organise it the way you want it be.

My people shall be satisfied with my goodness,
saith the Lord.
Jeremiah 31:14

Thy word have I his in mine heart that I might
not sin against Thee.
Psalm 119:11

O that the world might know
The all-atoning Lamb
Spirit of faith, descend and show
The virtue of His name.

Crystal: Black Tourmaline
Colour: Black
Oil: Lemongrass

Guide of the Day:
Don't look a gift horse in the mouth. Someone is offering you something good. Take it. Don't wait or else it could disappear as quickly as it came. Think of what it takes to make a rainbow in the sky. It has to be raining and the sun must be shining at just the right angle. The

conditions need to right otherwise we would see rainbows every day.

As thy day, so shall thy strength be.
Deuteronomy 33:25

Truly my soul waiteth upon God, from Him cometh my salvation.
Psalm 62:1

Do not look at life's long sorrow,
See how small each moments pain
God will help thee for tormented
Every day begins again.

Crystal: Chalcopyrite
Colour: Yellow-Green
Oil: Sage

Guide of the Day:
As you have much material wealth around even if you do not think it, you do. You have something precious in your life and all around you. You have something precious inside you too. Accept the gift of love and love yourself. Treat yourself to a gift, buy those shoes, and

wear that dress. You deserve it give yourself the greatest gift; love.

If we ask anything according to His will, He heareth as.
1 John 5:14

Hear, O Lord, and have mercy on me, Lord be Thou my helper.
Psalm 30:10

My times are in Thy hand;
My God, I wish them there
My life, my soul, my all I leave
Entirely to Thy care.

Crystal: Staurolite/Fairy Tears
Colour: Brown
Oil: Chamomile

Guide of the Day:
You need to be strong and stay strong in all that you do. It is time now to buckle down and get with the job. Hard work is called for in preparation for the good times ahead.

The God of Jacob is our refuge.
Psalm 46:7

I will not let Thee go except Thou bless me.
Genesis 32:26

Should earth lose its foundation,
He stand my lasting Rock
No temporal desolation
Shall give my love a shock.

Crystal: Red Jasper
Colour: Red
Oil: Dragon's Blood

Guide of the Day:

This is a period of intense action and hard work. Yet you will have family and friends around you to support you in your endeavours and it all be for the greater good. Life and work in particular may present you with many trials at present but your strength and determination will shine through.

We know that all things work together for good
to them that love God.
Romans 8:28

My soul followeth hard after Thee; Thy right
hand upholdeth me.
Psalm 63:8

All Things, there is no thread of woe
Too dark, too tangled for the bright design,
No drop of rain too heavy for the bow
Set in the cloud in covenant divine.

Crystal: Prasiolite
Colour: Green
Oil: Peppermint

<u>Guide of the Day:</u>
Hard work is something you are not frightened off and you outshine others when you put your mind to a task. A bit of elbow grease is called for and you are ready.

The Lord is with you while ye be with Him.
2 Chronicles 15:2

I have set the Lord, always before me.
Psalm 16:8

In fellowship I'd walk with Thee,
Thy sufferings Lord to share
Would know Thy resurrection power,
Daily Thy cross to bear.

Crystal: Platinum
Colour: Silver
Oil: Pine

Guide of the Day:

You have so many things you need to do and so many places you need to go that you feel thin. You feel drawn out causing a rift in yourself or subsequently a relationship as you realise some one is putting too many demands on you. Ask your angels for strength and get through this day.

For He saith to Moses, I will have mercy on whom I still have mercy.
Romans 9:15

Consider and hear me, O Lord my God.
Psalm 13:3

And while as a stranger I sojourn below,
The covenant blessing, Lord freely bestow.

Crystal: Blue Topaz
Colour: Blue
Oil: Eucalyptus

Guide of the Day:
Unfortunately, we do not have a clone and most of us cannot astral project ourselves to do one job while our bodies do something else. Learn to say no and see who it is that is placing so many demands upon you. You might be surprised.

The Lord will perfect that which concerneth me.
Psalm 138:8

Lord, lift thou up the Light of thy countenance upon us.
Psalm 4:6

His hope supports us here,
It makes our burdens light,
It serves our drooping heart to cheer
Till faith shall end in sight.

Crystal: Edenite
Colour: Green
Oil: Bay

Guide of the Day:
You are coming out of the darkness and into the light. At times, we cannot see the darkness surrounding us as we have grown so accustomed to it. We think that this is the norm. That this is the way life is meant to be. But it is not.

My strength is made perfect in weakness.
2 Corinthians 12:1

Cause me to know the way wherein I should walk.
Psalm 143:8

We have no strength to meet
The storms that round us lower;
Keep Thou our trembling feet
In every trying hour.

Crystal: Rhodonite
Colour: Pale Pink
Oil: Magnolia

Guide of the Day:
Embrace the good that is coming your way as you deserve it. Go out and treat yourself. It can be anything from a new dress to a new car, even a single flower. Just give yourself a little treat by acknowledging you survived the storm and you are now free of it all.

And they shall walk with me in white, for they are worthy.
Revelations 3:4

Wash me and I shall be whiter than snow.
Psalm 51:7

Lo! these are they from sufferings great
Who come to realms of light,
And in the blood of Christ have washed
These robes which shine so bright.

Crystal: Andean Opal
Colour: White
Oil: Honeysuckle

Guide of the Day:
The sadness and darkness has gone or it will be gone within the next five weeks. You will not know yourself soon now that the weight has been lifted. The storm is well and truly over.

I go to prepare a place for you.
John 14:2

Whom have I in heaven but Thee.
Psalm 73:25

Before the throne of God above,
I have a strong, a perfect plea;
A great High Priest whose name is love,
Whoever lives and pleads for me.

Crystal: Blue Fluorite
Colour: Blue
Oil: Wisteria

Guide of the Day:
You need to connect with your sense of wonder and find your innocence once more. There is also nostalgia for someone or something from your childhood, who may even make an appearance.

The Lord is merciful and gracious.
Psalm 103:8

Have mercy upon me and hear my prayers.
Psalm 4:1

My God how excellent Thy grace!
Whence all our hope and comfort springs,
The Sons of Adam in distress
Fly to the shelter of Thy wings.

Crystal: Amethyst
Colour: Purple
Oil: Lavender

Guide of the Day:

The dawn of a new day brings opportunity of new beginnings of projects close to your heart. What you plan in doing pay attention to when you are doing it. As plans need detail but they also need timing. All the best laid plans in the world can unfold if the timing is not right. So, plan and get the details right but also get the timing right. Choose your moment wisely as it can determine whether your project will be a success.

He shall call upon me and I will answer Him.
Psalm 91:15

Be merciful unto me, O Lord for I cry unto Thee daily.
Psalm 86:3

With boldness therefore, at the Throne
Let us make our sorrows know,
And seek the aid of Heavenly power
To help us in each trying hour.

Crystal: Sardonyx
Colour: Brown
Oil: Musk

Guide of the Day:
Begin to find out about your family and begin the search for your family tree. A hobby and past time that is rewarding and intriguing. Find the heroes and sinners in your family. Search for them in different lands and build a family tree with dates and information about them.

And while they are yet speaking I will hear.
Isaiah 65:24

Shew us Thy mercy, O Lord and grant us Thy Salvation.
Psalm 85:7

A dying risen Jesus,
Seen by the eye of faith
At once from anguish free us,
And saves the Soul from death.

Crystal: Ruby
Colour: Red
Oil: Rose

Guide of the Day:
All may not be what it seems and the grass many not be as green. So, stop where you are and think about it. This ladder of opportunity appears for about six weeks so it is up to you if you want to step onto the ladder and do the work that is involved to get where you want to be.

Behold, God is my salvation; I will trust and not be afraid.
Isaiah 12:2

Help me, O Lord my God, O same me according to Thy mercy.
Psalm 109:26

Jesus, Thy blood and righteousness
My beauty is, my glowing dress;
Mid flowing worlds in these arrayed
With joy shall I lift up my head.

Crystal: Turquoise
Colour: Blue
Oil: Iris

Guide of the Day:
Whatever it is that is on its way whether positive or negative it is the result of past actions so think of karma what goes around comes back around. If you have been wronged in the past then you will be exonerated and your star shall rise.

My grace is sufficient for thee.
2 Corinthians 12:9

Be thou, O Lord, art a shield for me.
Psalm 3:3

There is a certainty of love
That sets my heart at rest;
A calm assurance for to-day
That what He gives is best.

Crystal: Red Jasper
Colour: Red
Oil: Cinnamon

Guide of the Day:
You have the chance to change the course of direction if you wish. In many times in our lives we change direction. In years' past people trained in one profession which stayed with them for the rest of their lives. Today it is useful to have two or even three professions behind you for example from teacher to carpenter, to

decorator. We can never be too sure of our professions anymore.

I will not leave you comfortless.
John 14:18

Let I pray thee thy merciful kindness be for my comfort.
Psalm 119:76

For thee thy Saviour's prayer shall yet prevail,
Thy faith in Him though weak, shall never fail.

Crystal: Chrysocolla
Colour: Blue/Turquoise
Oil: Lotus

Guide of the Day:
Believe in the wonder of the world around you and with the eyes of a child look again at the world with innocence and fragile wonder. Believe in the potential of fairies and unicorns.

There is that maketh himself poor, yet hath great riches.
Proverbs 13:7

Thanks, be to God which giveth us the victory through our Lord Jesus Christ.
1 Corinthians 15:57

Thrice blest is he to whom is given
The instinct that can tell
That God in on the field when He is most invisible.

Crystal: Seriphos Quartz
Colour: Green
Oil: Thyme

Guide of the Day:
You may be over sensitive towards a situation and you are allowing your emotions to rule your head. Give yourself some breathing space and count to ten before you react in a way that could prove detrimental to the future outcome.

A blessing if ye obey the commandments of the Lord your God.
Deuteronomy 11:27

Lord, I believe; help Thou mine unbelief.
Mark 9:24

Ah! the heart that is contended
Nought to know save God alone,
In the fullness of His blessing,
Finds a peace before unknown.

Crystal: Oligoclase
Colour: White
Oil: Jasmine

<u>Guide of the Day:</u>
Our emotions are tied to the natural rhythms of the moon and oceans as we are all connected. Yet try to be relaxed in certain situations and do not let your emotions get in the way or you seeing the true reality in front of you.

I will come again and receive you unto myself.
John 14:3

With my whole heart have I sought Thee.
Psalm 119:10

Rejoice! Rejoice! ye happy band
Of pilgrims bound for heaven;
For mercies, countless as the sand
Have to your soul's been given.

Crystal: Jade
Colour: Green
Oil: Basil

Guide of the Day:
You have placed your dreams, ambition, and destiny on the clock of 9 to 5. Find a way to live true to your destiny. Take a class or course after work in what you wanted to learn. Volunteer on your days off in a place where you wanted to work. Begin to put your dreams into reality and get your destiny back on track.

Your sins are forgiven you for His name's sake.
1 John 2:12

Preserve me, O God, for in Thee do I put my trust.
Psalm 16:1

Through Christ alone we live; for He
Hath drowned our transgressions all
In Love's unfathomable sea,
O Love, unknown, unsearchable!

Crystal: Generator Quartz
Colour: White
Oil: Bergamot

Guide of the Day:
You need to develop a back bone and stand up for yourself in a situation. Do not allow anyone to bully or intimidate you. Expose the bully and shed light on to the lie or bullies, as all lies and bullies hate the light as it goes against what they stand for.

He heareth the prayer of the righteous.
Proverbs 15:29

Lord save us; we perish.
Mathew 8:25

Give me, Lord, Thy gentle heart,
Lowliness my portion be,
Mark Redeemer, now impart
Thine own humility.

Crystal: Grounding Quartz
Colour: White
Oil: Narcissus

Guide of the Day:
Yet you are a warrior for the greater good and you have the strength, a back bone that runs along with justice. So, stand up for your rights and fight for yourself and for the ones who do not have a voice of their own.

A man shall be as rivers of water in a dry place.
Isaiah 32:2

I direct my prayer unto Thee, and will look up.
Psalm 5:3

Lord, we are rivers running to Thy sea,
Our waves and ripples all derived from Thee;
A nothing we should have, a nothing be,
Except for Thee.

Crystal: Banded Agate
Colour: Cream/Ivory
Oil: Mimosa

Guide of the Day:
Something that you desire badly is just out of reach to you. You are reaching so badly for it you might slip and fall. You could lose everything as a result. So, do not over extend your reach longer than you can reduce it. Sometimes things just are out of our reach. Be careful in the process not to miss out on things that you have right in front of you.

I have prayed for thee that thy faith fail not.
Luke 22:32

Think upon me, my God, for good.
Nehemiah 5:19

O let that faith which Thou has taught
Be treasured in my breast
The evidence of unseen joys
The substance of our rest.

Crystal: Healer's Gold
Colour: Gold
Oil: Myrrh

Guide of the Day:
We all make mistakes but accepting others mistakes is difficult especially when they can hurt us. Learn to forgive and ask your angels for guidance in forgiving and forgetting.

I will give unto them eternal life.
John 10:28

O God be not far from me.
Psalm 71:22

How blest are they who still abide?
Close sheltered in Thy bleeding side!
Who life and strength from Thee derive,
And by Thee move and in Thee live.

Crystal: Marble
Colour: Grey
Oil: Thyme

Guide of the Day:
It's okay if everything goes wrong; you get to work late, traffic is terrible, your boss was horrible to you. Everyone has good and bad days. Find something to make you laugh and put a smile on your face.

The Lord is thy keeper; the Lord is thy shade upon thy right hand.
Psalm 121:5

Lord, who shall abide in Thy Tabernacle?
Psalm 15:1

Jehovah keepeth thee! and upon thy right hand Jevovah, as thy shade doth ever near thee stand.

Crystal: Aquamarine
Colour: Aqua
Oil: Peppermint

Guide of the Day:
Believe in miracles today and look for signs everywhere.

Call upon me in the day of trouble; I will deliver thee.
Psalm 50:15

O God, in the multitude of Thy mercy hear me.
Psalm 69:13

For even the silent breathings
Of the spirit raised above
Shall reach His throne of glory
Who is Mercy, Truth and Love.

Crystal: Amber
Colour: Orange
Oil: Amber

<u>Guide of the Day:</u>
Tell someone your love them today.

Faithful is he that calleth you, who also will do it.

Thessalonians 5:24

Have mercy upon me, O Lord, for I am weak.

Psalm 6:2

Arise, my soul from deep distress
And banish every fear;
God calls thee to His throne of Grace,
To spread thy sorrow there.

Crystal: Jet
Colour: Black
Oil: Myrrh

Guide of the Day:
Don't dwell on the negative today. People behave in strange ways where love is concerned.

And I will dwell among the children of Israel,
and will be their God.
Exodus 29:45

Teach me to Thy will for thou art my God.
Psalm 143:10

From every stormy wind that blows
From every swelling tide of woes
There is a calm, a safe retreat -
Tis found beneath the mercy seat.

Crystal: Bronzite
Colour: Brown
Oil: Ginger

Guide of the Day

Give a compliment today and tell someone their hair looks good or their clothes look nice. Make someone's day by being thoughtful.

Therefore, will the Lord want that He may be gracious unto you.
Isaiah 30:18

My heart shall rejoice in thy salvation.
Psalm 13:5

Thy mercy-seat is open still
There let my soul retreat
With humble hope attend thy will
And waith beneath Thy feet.

Crystal: Rutilated Quartz
Colour: Gold
Oil: Cinnamon

Guide of the Day:
Sometimes you just have to cut your losses and leave. It can be frightening starting again but you have all the tools and experiences you need to succeed this time.

For by grace are ye saved through Faith.
Ephesians 2:8

Keep me as the apple of the eye.
Psalm 17:8

The Holy Lamb for sin was slain
The sinners endless life might gain.

Crystal: Aqua Aura
Colour: Blue
Oil: Lavender

Guide of the Day:
Do not rush today, take your time and try to leave early to wherever you are going.

The God of love and peace shall be with you.
2 Corinthians 13:11

O God; Thou art my help and my deliverer.
Psalm 70:5

Apart from Thee all gain is loss
All labour vainly done;
The solemn shadow of the Cross
Is better than the sun.

Crystal: Selenite
Colour: White
Oil: Eucalyptus

Guide of the Day:
Life is short so live it by doing what you love.

The eyes of the Lord are upon the righteous.
Psalm 34:15

Shew me Thy ways, O Lord, teach me Thy paths.
Psalm 25:4

Enough to know that I am Thine
And precious Saviour, Thou art mine
Thou canst not err - Thou wilt not leave,
Nor willingly Thy servant grieve.

Crystal: Tektite
Colour: Charcoal Grey
Oil: Cloves

Guide of the Day:
At times, certain news can knock us back and we are terrified of the end result. Ask your angels for help and guidance.

Peace I leave with you, my peace I give unto you.
John 14:27

Peace be with you all that are in Christ Jesus.
1 Peter 5:14

Though Faith and hope awhile he tried
I ask not, need not aught beside
So, safe, so calm, so satisfied
In the soul that clings to Thee.

Crystal: Haematite
Colour: Silver
Oil: Allspice

Guide of the Day:
Find a job you love to do and you never work a day in your life.

The Lord is good unto them that wait for Him.
Lamentations 3:25

I waited patiently for the Lord, and He inclined unto me and heard my cry.
Psalm 40:1

Not so in haste, my heart.
Have faith in God and wait.
Although He linger long
Her never comes late.

Crystal: Turquoise
Colour: Turquoise
Oil: Lotus

Guide of the Day:
Look in the mirror and find something you like about yourself. Tell that face in the mirror you love them.

He will fulfil the desire of them that fear Him.
Psalm 145:19

Lord, if Thou wilt, Thou canst make me clean.
Luke 5:12

Sweet to reflect how grace divine
My sins on Jesus laid;
Sweet to remember that His death
My debt of suffering paid.

Crystal: Angelite
Colour: Pale Blue
Oil: Peach

Guide of the Day:
Be respectful of people today and use your manners, say thank you whenever you can.

He hath made with me an everlasting covenant ordered in all things and sure.
2 Samuel 23:5

And with Thy blessing let the house of Thy servant be blessed for ever.
2 Samuel 7:29

O doubting one, the Eternal Three
Are pledged in faithfulness for thee
Claim every promise sweet and sure
By covenant oath of God secure.

Crystal: Blue Goldstone
Colour: Gold
Oil: Orchid

Guide of the Day:
Do not gossip today, remember the old saying, 'loose lips sink ships.' Do not say anything behind someone's back that you would not say to their face.

The people who do know their God shall be strong.
Daniel 11:32

O Lord; deliver my soul.
Psalm 6:4

Strong in Thy strength, tho' in myself but weakness,
Equal to all I know that I shall be.

Crystal: Sunshine Aura Quartz
Colour: Gold
Oil: Frankincense

Guide of the Day:
Do not put off tomorrow what you can do today.

I will strengthen thee; yea I will help thee.
Isaiah 4:10

But all those that put their trust in Thee rejoice.
Psalm 5:11

Strengthen my hand, O Lord, for I am weak
Thou art the strong one, Lord, Thy help I seek.

Crystal: Olive Jade
Colour: Green
Oil: Olive

Guide of the Day:
Everything has it's time and loss is a part of life. The hardest word we learn to say is goodbye.

I will give thee a crown of life.
Revelation 2:10

So, teach us to number our days, that we may apply our hearts unto wisdom.
Psalm 90:12

I see Him with pity down
And hold in view with conqueror's crown
Though pressed with grief and pain before
My soul revives and asks for more.

Crystal: Amethyst
Colour: Purple
Oil: Patchouli

Guide of the Day:
Rest up and relax today, store your energy. It's good just for once to do absolutely nothing.

I will pour upon him that is thirsty.
Isaiah 44:3

Incline thine ear unto me; in the day when I call answer me speedily.
Psalm 102:2

See from the rock the waters bursting
In copious streams at God's command,
His people to refresh when thirsting,
With fresh supplies from His own hand.

Crystal: Shiva Lingam
Colour: Cream
Oil: Magnolia

Guide of the Day:
Turn off the T.V. switch off the phone and leave the computer off. Sit and listen to the sounds of the day and go for a walk-in nature.

Whoso hearkeneth unto me shall dwell safely.
Proverb 1:33

Lead us not into temptation.
Mathew 6:13

Man of sorrows, what a name
For the Son of God who came,
Ruined sinners to reclaim,
What a mighty Saviour!

Crystal: Rock Frankincense
Colour: Gold
Oil: Myrrh

Guide of the Day:
Put your faith in the universe today and do what you have always wanted.

The Lord shall guide thee continually.
Isaiah 58:33

Let the words of my mouth and the meditation of my heart be acceptable.
Psalm 19:14

Come to the throne of grace,
Now in your utmost need;
Spread all before your Father's face,
His word of promise plead.

Crystal: Green Zircon
Colour: Green
Oil: Basil

<u>Guide of the Day:</u>

Today remember those who have passed and celebrate their lives even if it not an anniversary. Light a blue candle and give thanks for their lives and for their eternal peace.

The Lord of Hosts is with us; God of Jacob is our refuge.
Psalm 46:7

Hear me, O Lord, for Thy loving-kindness is good.
Psalm 69: 16

O Lord, assist me through the fight.
Make me triumphant in Thy might,
Then the desponding heart cast raise,
The victory mine and Thine the praise.

Crystal: Twin Quartz
Colour: White
Oil: Anise

Guide of the Day:
Think about what your idea of what home and family means to you and what it should look like. Make your living environment a priority today and spruce it up.

And lo, I am with you always, even unto the end
of the world.
Mathew 28:20

I beseech thee show me thy glory.
Exodus 33:18

Lord, make one with Thine own fanciful ones
The saints who love Thee, and one loved by
Thee;
Till the day break and all the shadows flee.

Crystal: Blue Sapphire
Colour: Blue
Oil: Orchid

Guide of the Day:
Think about those loved ones who are away from home today and give them a phone call or write them a letter to show them how much you care.

The joy of the Lord is your strength.
Nehemiah 8:10

That I may know Him and the fellowship of His sufferings.
Philippians 3:10

I welcome then with heart sincere,
The Cross my Saviour bids me take;
No lead, no trial is severe,
That's borne or suffered for His sake.

Crystal: Ajoite Quartz
Colour: Turquoise
Oil: Sandalwood

Guide of the Day:
Make sure you let people know your boundaries today. We want people to treat us with respect as we do them.

He hath chosen us in Him before the foundation of the world.
Ephesians 1:4

Give me understanding and I shall keep thy law.
Psalm 119:34

Chosen by His own good pleasure, by the counsel of His will,
Mystery of power and wisdom working for His people still.

Crystal: White Moonstone
Colour: Silver
Oil: Eucalyptus

Guide of the Day:
Take a light approach to a remark today and just brush it off to someone's inexperience of life.

Fear not, for I have redeemed thee; I have called thee by thy name.
Isaiah 43:1

I pray Thee, if I have found grace in Thy sight, show me now Thy way.
Exodus 33:13

Oft when I seem to tread alone
Some barren waste with thorns o'ergrown
Thy voice of love in tenderest tone,
Whispers - still trust in me.

Crystal: Gold Sheen Obsidian
Colour: Gold
Oil: Sandalwood

Guide of the Day:
Let your hidden talent out today and shine like the star you are.

For Thy light is come.
Isaiah 60:1

O God, Thou art my God, early will I seek Thee.
Psalm 63:1

I will think of what Jesus hath done,
I will think of what yet He will do,
And I know that through painful my path
He will bring me triumphantly through.

Crystal: Sardonyx
Colour: Brown
Oil: Musk

<u>Guide of the Day:</u>
Change is unstoppable and even the most difficult times will pass no matter how devastating they may seem.

If we suffer we shall also reign with Him.
2 Timothy 2:12

But I have trusted in Thy mercy.
Psalm 13:5

My time of suffering and distress
Has proved my Lord's abounding grace;
Now that He chastens but to bless
This I clearly trace.

Crystal: Amethyst
Colour: Purple
Oil: Amethyst

Guide of the Day:
Let go of anything that is no good for you, or anything that no longer suits you, or is broken. Throw out the garbage and make a fresh way and room in your life.

I will restore health unto thee, and I will heal
thee of thy words.
Jeremiah 30:17

O spare me, that I may recover strength before I
go hence.
Psalm 39:13

Lord, though Thou bend my spirit low,
Love only shall I see;
The very hand that strikes the blow
Was wounded once for me.

Crystal: Spirit Quartz
Colour: Gold
Oil: Myrrh

Guide of the Day:
Try to find a balance with nature today and your own nature.

And He said, my presence shall go with thee.
Exodus 33:14

In Thy presence is fulness of joy.
Psalm 16:11

O how blessed are the moments
When the Lord Himself draws near,
When I feel his gracious presence
And He listens to my prayer.

Crystal: Franlinite
Colour: Terracotta
Oil: Ginger

Guide of the Day:
Try to meditate today and if you cannot meditate then do something that will make you concentrate on the outcome such as colouring using limited colours. Create a pattern using only three colours.

Thou hast holden my by my right hand.
Psalm 73:23

Teach me, O Lord, the way of Thy statutes.
Psalm 119:33

While yet I journey through this weary land
Keep me from wondering, Father take my hand.

Crystal: Novaculite
Colour: Grey
Oil: Lavender

Guide of the Day:
Try to develop your intuition today and listen to your inner voice.

And he that reapeth receiveth wages and gathereth fruit unto eternal life.
John 4:36

Thou has been my help, therefore in the shadow of Thy wings will I rejoice.
Psalm 63:7

When from the dust of death, I rise
To take my mansion in the skies,
E'en then shall this be all my plea -
Jesus hath lived and died for me.

Crystal: Haematite
Colour: Silver
Oil: Dragon's Blood

Guide of the Day:
Strengthen your resolve and your resilience today you are going to need it in the coming days.

For this God is our God, for ever and ever.
Psalm 48:14

If thou wilt tho canst make me clean.
Mark 1:40

O faithless, unbelieving heart,
So, slow to trust thy tenderest Friend,
Who will all needful strength impart,
An loving, love thee to the end.

Crystal: Neptunite
Colour: Green
Oil: Lime

Guide of the Day:
Time for a change whether it be heart or home.
Make the decision you have been putting off.

Books of the Bible

Here are the names of the Old and New Testament Books arranged in their order they appear in the Bible.

The Books of the Old Testament

Genesis
Exodus
Leviticus
Numbers
Deuteronomy
Joshua
Judges
Ruth
1 Samuel
2 Samuel
1 Kings
2 Kings
1 Chronicles
2 Chronicles
Ezra
Nehemiah
Esther
Job
Psalms

Proverbs
Ecclesiastes
Song of Solomon
Isaiah
Jeremiah
Lamentations
Ezekiel
Daniel
Hosea
Joel
Amos
Obadiah
Jonah
Micah
Nahum
Habakkuk
Zephaniah
Haggai
Zechariah
Malachi

The Books of the New Testament
Mathew
Mark
Luke

John
The Acts
Romans
1 Corinthians
2 Corinthians
Galatians
Ephesians
Philippians
Colossians
1 Thessalonians
2 Thessalonians
1 Timothy
2 Timothy
Titus
Philemon
Hebrews
James
1 Peter
2 Peter
1 John
2 John
3 John
Jude
Revelation

Bible Books Used

Here is a list of the books of the bible used in this book. This reference shows the number of the passage found in the bible. The first number is the chapter of that book and the second number is the verse. All promise and prayers here in this book are written as they appear in the box of scrolls.
The books appear here in alphabetical order.

Acts 7:60

Acts 9:6

Acts 10:43

2 Chronicles 15:2

1 Corinthians 3: 22-23

1 Corinthians 15:57

2 Corinthians 1:20

2 Corinthians 6:16

2 Corinthians 12:1

2 Corinthians 12:9

2 Corinthians 13:7

2 Corinthians 13:11

Daniel 9:3

Daniel 11:32

Deuteronomy 7:6

Deuteronomy 11:27
Deuteronomy 30:20
Deuteronomy 33:25
Deuteronomy 33:27
Ecclesiastes 3:14
Ephesians 1:4
Ephesians 2:8
Exodus 3:12
Exodus 29:45
Exodus 33:13
Exodus 33:14
Exodus 33:18
Ezekiel 36:26
Ezekiel 36:27
Genesis 9:14
Genesis 32:26
Genesis 49:18
Haggai 2:4
Hebrews 13:5
Isaiah 4:10
Isaiah 12:2
Isaiah 25:4
Isaiah 26:4
Isaiah 26:12
Isaiah 30:18

Isaiah 32:2
Isaiah 32:18
Isaiah 33:16
Isaiah 33:17
Isaiah 37:17
Isaiah 38:14
Isaiah 38:17
Isaiah 40:31
Isaiah 41:10
Isaiah 43:1
Isaiah 43:3
Isaiah 44:3
Isaiah 49:2
Isaiah 49:16
Isaiah 54:17
Isaiah 58:33
Isaiah 60:1
Isaiah 65:19
Isaiah 65:25
Jeremiah 1:8
Jeremiah 3:12
Jeremiah 9:24
Jeremiah 15:21
Jeremiah 24:7
Jeremiah 30:11

Jeremiah 30:17
Jeremiah 31:3
Jeremiah 31:14
Jeremiah 32:40
Jeremiah 37:20
Job 27:6
John 2:17
John 4:36
John 10:28
John 12:26
John 14:2
John 14:3
John 14:14
John 14:16
John 14:18
John 14:27
John 16:24
1 John 2:12
1 John 5:14
Jonah 2:2
Judges 16:28
Lamentations 3:25
Luke 5:12
Luke 8:48
Luke 22:32

Luke 23:46
Malachi 3:17
Malachi 4:2
Mark 1:40
Mark 9:24
Mathew 1:21
Mathew 6:13
Mathew 8:25
Mathew 9:27
Mathew 11:28
Mathew 14:27
Mathew 25:46
Mathew 28:20
Nahum 1:7
Nehemiah 5:19
Nehemiah 8:10
Philippians 1:6
Philippians 3:10
Philippians 4:19
Proverbs 1:33
Proverbs 3:26
Proverbs 4:18
Proverbs 11:25
Proverbs 14:26
Proverbs 15:29

1 Peter 5:4

1 Peter 5:10

1 Peter 5:14

Revelation 2:7

Revelation 2:10

Revelation 3:4

Revelation 21:4

Revelation 22:5

Romans 8:28

Romans 9:12

1 Samuel 3:10

2 Samuel 7:29

2 Samuel 23:5

Thessalonians 5:24

1 Thessalonians 4:17

2 Timothy 2:12

2 Timothy 4:18

Titus 2:14

Book of Psalms

There are 150 Psalms in the Bible. They form the majority of prayers and promises in the Book of Scrolls. The Psalms are a wonderful book to read and learn from. Although the majority of the Psalms are principally written by David some of the Psalms are inspired by angels. The Archangel Michael is accredited with writing Psalm 85. The Psalms themselves were intended to be sung to music as the word Psalms actually means songs. The Psalms were probably written over a period of 1000 years and reveal the piety and devotion of the truly religious in Israel. The Psalms touch upon every human experience and give hope to all who read them.

Here is a list of the Psalms used in The Book of Scrolls:

Psalm 3:3

Psalm 3:7

Psalm 4:1

Psalm 4:6

Psalm 4:8

Psalm 5:1

Psalm 5:3

Psalm 5:8

Psalm 5:11

Psalm 5:12

Psalm 6:2

Psalm 6:4

Psalm 6:9

Psalm 13:3

Psalm 13:5

Psalm 15:1

Psalm 16:1

Psalm 16:5
Psalm 16:8
Psalm 16:11
Psalm 17.5
Psalm 17:8
Psalm 20:4
Psalm 22:11
Psalm 23:1
Psalm 23:6
Psalm 25:4
Psalm 25:11
Psalm 26:8
Psalm 27:9
Psalm 27:11
Psalm 29:11
Psalm30:10
Psalm 31:5
Psalm 32:7
Psalm 32:8
Psalm 32:16
Psalm 33:18
Psalm 34:15
Psalm 34:22
Psalm 35:3
Psalm 37:24

Psalm 37:39
Psalm 37:40
Psalm 39:13
Psalm 40:1
Psalm 40:8
Psalm 40:10
Psalm 41:3
Psalm 41:4
Psalm 46:7
Psalm 48:14
Psalm 50:15
Psalm 51:2
Psalm 51:3
Psalm 51:7
Psalm 51:9
Psalm 51:11
Psalm 51:12
Psalm 51:15
Psalm 52:8
Psalm 54:2
Psalm 54:6
Psalm 55:1
Psalm 56:11
Psalm 61:4
Psalm 62:1

Psalm 63:1
Psalm 63:7
Psalm 63:8
Psalm 65:11
Psalm 67:1
Psalm 68:10
Psalm 69:13
Psalm 69:16
Psalm 70:5
Psalm 71:22
Psalm 73:23
Psalm 73:25
Psalm 80:2
Psalm 85:7
Psalm 86:3
Psalm 86:4
Psalm 86:7
Psalm 86:11
Psalm 86:16
Psalm 90:12
Psalm 90:14
Psalm 90:15
Psalm 91:3
Psalm 91:11
Psalm 91:15

Psalm 102:1
Psalm 102:2
Psalm 103:4
Psalm 103:8
Psalm 107:6
Psalm 109:20
Psalm 119:8
Psalm 119:10
Psalm 119:11
Psalm 119:18
Psalm 119:28
Psalm 119:33
Psalm 119:34
Psalm 119:36
Psalm 119:67
Psalm 119:71
Psalm 119:76
Psalm 119:80
Psalm 119:94
Psalm 121:5
Psalm 121:6
Psalm 121:7
Psalm 138:7
Psalm 138:8
Psalm 139:11

Psalm 139:17
Psalm 139:23
Psalm 139:24
Psalm 141:8
Psalm 143:8
Psalm 145:10
Psalm 145:19

Language of Angels Course

The Language of Angels Course can be found at the British College of Witchcraft and Wizardry:

www.thebritishcollegeofwitchcraftandwizardry.org

The Language of Angels

Find Out More

About This Course

Probably the only series of courses of their kind anywhere in the world today, THE LANGUAGE OF ANGELS SERIES is specifically designed for Earth Angels and those wishing to learn the practical aspects of communicating with Angels.

Who Should Study This Course?
Because it is the first in a complete series of

courses, PART 1 is suitable for anyone wishing to develop a practical working knowledge of Angel communication in all its forms. Ideally suited for both Healers and Earth Angels, this course is available to anyone and will provide a good induction to the College and the work that we do..

Course Objectives:

1. To learn the different ways to actually communicate with Angels one-to-one.
2. To gain the best possible results from asking angels for help and advice.
3. To learn which angel to communicate with for different needs and objectives.
4. To learn the correspondences for each angel and what they mean.

5. To learn to correctly communicate with and ask for help in the literal language of Angels as given to us millennia ago, AND as used by initiates down through the ages.

Programme Delivery:

Delivered entirely online through our Online Classroom and includes individual tutor support. You will receive password access to the dedicated online College Learning Area and course classroom. Within the Classroom are contained all of the course Modules which the individual Lessons, audio and where appropriate video tutorials, comprehensive instruction, techniques, learning modules and a student support notice board. Everything is specifically designed for you to learn effectively online in the comfort of your own home, and in your own time.

Course Teaching Methods:

Online delivery, online support, online resources with direct access to tutors for personal support where required. Series of 12 modules with 25 lessons, course materials and appropriate downloads. Interactive notice board for students to raise questions and to discussion points. Lessons will have tasks, assignments and activity for students to complete as they progress through the course.

Course Equipment:

1. Copy of King James Bible
2. An Angel Book - This is a simple exercise book which can be anything from a small note

book to a diary. It is for your personal use only. It is to be used for recording your Angel encounters and Angel work in. Including the gifts the Angels may leave you without your awareness.

3. Copy of the The Language of Angels, however, each lesson will come complete with its own course materials including the Psalm and any other spiritual scripture needed.

Outline of Course:

Lesson 1

1. Angels
2. Who, what, how - A brief history on the Angels.
3. Angels all around us - we all have a personal Angel who walks with us.

4. The gifts Angels leave us - Angels may have been trying to contact you without you realizing.

5. Tasks

6. Find our who your Angel is.

Lesson 2

1. Protection

2. How to differentiate between light and negative Angels

3. How to communicate safely with the Angels. (Similar to the Green Cross Code. Think of Angel Language as the White Cross Code.)

Lesson 3

1. The Archangels

2. Who they are, and their importance.

3. How to communicate with the Elohim at their level

Lesson 4

1. Language and Correspondences.
2. The time, day, colours, incense, crystals and oils of Angels to be used.

Lesson 5

1. Angels, language for communications pertaining to love and relationships including friendships.

Lesson 6

1. Angels, language and communications regarding business, including financial help and legal enterprises.

Lesson 7

1. Angels, language and communications regarding health, including physical, emotional and spiritual health.

Lesson 8

1. Angels, language, and communications pertaining to protection including different forms of travel.

Lesson 9

1. Angels, language, and different forms of communication regarding luck including eliminating bad luck and ensuring good luck.

Lesson 10

1. Angels, language, and different forms of communication regarding career including choosing the right one and listening to what your Angel has to say on the matter.

Lesson 11

1. Angels, language and communications with guidance and for the protection of the Animal Kingdom.

Lesson 12

1. Angels, language and communications pertaining to the health of the world including spiritual health of all peoples.
2. Light workers level of consciousness.
3. The universal interaction of love.
4. Formative Assessment

How to apply for a place on this course:

To register for this program, simply visit:

www.thebritishcollegeofwitchcraftandwizardry.org